The Gospel of John and the Sociology of Light

Language and Characterization in the Fourth Gospel

Norman R. Petersen

WIPF & STOCK · Eugene, Oregon

Wipf and Stock Publishers
199 W 8th Ave, Suite 3
Eugene, OR 97401

The Gospel of John and the Sociology of Light
Language and Characterization in the Fourth Gospel
By Petersen, Norman R.
Copyright©1993 by Petersen, Norman R.
ISBN 13: 978-1-60608-114-3
Publication date 8/1/2008
Previously published by Trinity Press International, 1993

To George W. E. Nickelsburg
and
Birger A. Pearson,
friends

Contents

Contents

Introduction

My kingship is not of this world.   18:36a

*He who is of the earth belongs to the earth, and of the earth
he speaks; he who comes from heaven bears witness to what
he has seen and heard. For he whom God has sent utters the
words of God.*   3:31–34

No man ever spoke like this man!   7:46

*I have said this to you in figures; the hour is coming when I
shall no longer speak to you in figures but tell you plainly of
the Father.*   16:25

Ah, now you are speaking plainly, not in any figures! 16:29

One of the most distinctive features of the Gospel of John is its
blatantly self-conscious use of language. Everyone in the narrative, including the narrator, speaks everyday language, but the
narrator and Jesus also speak what we will call a special language,[1] one that employs the grammar and vocabulary of the
everyday but uses the vocabulary in a very different way, leading to misunderstandings and partial understandings on the
part of those who only speak the everyday language. The two
uses of language therefore contribute to the characterization of
both Jesus and those with whom he speaks, and because his
speech leads to his being rejected by some, and eventually to his
arrest and execution, the two uses of language also contribute to

1

the plot of John's story. What is more, because the uses of language correspond to different groups, such as the disciples and the Jews in the time of Jesus and the narrator and his people in later times, the use of the language also differentiates social groups within John's narrative world, groups that in all probability represent John's understanding of actual social distinctions in the real world in which he and his people lived.

Anyone familiar with Johannine studies will recognize that this description of the role of language in the fourth gospel does not contain much that is very new. For in one connection or another, other critics have made the same points. On the other hand, a knowing reader will also recognize that others have not put all of these points together in a single statement or a single study. For example, there have been a number of specialized studies of double or multiple meanings, of dualities, of irony, of metaphor, and of symbol as literary devices related to problems of understanding and/or to John's style of thought.[2] These studies, however, have not arrived at the same point as other critics, who have identified in one way or another what I referred to as a special language that is contrasted with everyday language, and who have seen these uses of language as representative of opposed linguistic communities.[3] And last, there have been yet other studies concerned with the history of the Johannine community and the social world in which it evolved, although these studies tend to make little of the role of language use.[4]

The present study is indebted in varying degrees to all of these efforts, but it differs from them because it attempts to bring together literary, linguistic, and social issues into a unified conception. This conception is based on the uses of language in John's narrative as we now have it, and it moves from this usage to John's system of characterization and then to the social world in which the characters act, both as individuals and as members of groups inhabiting the world represented in John's narrative. The conception is therefore a fundamentally literary one, although in the last two chapters we will have to venture outside of John into some comparative matters concerning Moses and the Jewish figure of the personified Wisdom (Sophia) of God. In both cases, we will draw some few historical inferences about the role of the images of Moses and Sophia in the social context in which John wrote. Even here, however, our concern will be largely literary, for our ultimate goal is to understand what John was saying and why he said it. In other words, we will not be concerned with trying to identify the exact historical context in and for which he was writing. That task calls for yet another project, one that entails going beyond the narrative as we have it and the sources of which it was composed, to the history of its composition, and to other historical information that is well known but still highly controversial.[5] I would like to think that if we are successful in accomplishing the task I have set out, we will make a contribution to this other one as well, if only by pointing to some historical implications of our literary observations.

The differences between our concerns and those of others also have consequences for the form of this study. Because of the nature of the differences I have described, I have chosen in the text of this book to focus solely on John's narrative, and to relegate to endnotes all references to other critics. This will make for a more readable text, one unencumbered by disruptive and possibly obfuscatory dialogue with others, while also providing an occasion for me to acknowledge my indebtedness and account for some of my differences. The notes, however, are not exhaustive; they only deal with matters I have found pertinent to problems we will encounter in John's narrative. I must leave it to another, braver soul, one more knowledgeable than I, to write what has yet to be written, namely a bibliographical essay on the use of language in the fourth gospel.[6] What then, are the problems we will encounter?

In Chapter 1, we will identify the basic characteristics of John's special use of everyday language by examining his own usage in the prologue to his narrative, John 1:1–18. We will find him creating synonyms out of terms that are not synonymous in everyday language, and we will identify a contrastive style of thinking and expression in his frequent use of semantic opposites and grammatical negations.[7] These characteristics raise the question of how we are to understand what he says, especially when he creates synonyms. We will find that because his synonymy blurs the referents of his language, what he says cannot be understood in terms of what his language refers to, but only, and in a limited way, in terms of the differences between what he says and what the users of the everyday language are saying when they use the same terms. Indeed, his language differs from the everyday because his people are different from the users of everyday language. Already in the prologue, the uses of language and the societies of the users are contrasted with one another in such a way as to shape the characters of those who belong to the two societies, which are comprised of those who accept Jesus and those who reject him. Moreover, it is precisely the character Jesus, as the Word become flesh and as the Light that has come into the world as the only Son from the Father, who creates this social and linguistic division by demanding that people respond to him.

In Chapters 2 and 3, we will focus on the relationship between language use and characterization, first in terms of *how* Jesus and others speak, and then in terms of *what* Jesus speaks about. Chapter 2, which is largely in the form of a commentary or reading of a sequence of several episodes, will deal with problems posed by play on double or multiple meanings, and by the use of irony, metaphor, and figurative versus plain speech, each of which results in misunderstandings by the speakers of everyday language, misunderstandings or inadequate ones that affect even the meaning of 'belief'. This chapter will go over ground covered by other critics, but while they were largely concerned with play *within* the possibilities of everyday language, we will also find, as some others have found, linguistic play *between* the everyday and John's special use of it, although I know of no study that considers all of these linguistic devices in terms of a Johannine special language.[8] The understanding of this special language gained from our study of the prologue will therefore put the results of previous studies in a new light.

The same is true for Chapter 3, because others have also observed both the multitude of identifiers used of Jesus (e.g., Son of God, Son of Man, prophet, Messiah, the Way, the Truth, and the Life) and the several different conceptual systems employed to represent his movement from heaven to earth, and sometimes back to heaven (e.g., the Son who was sent into the world by his Father and returns to him, the Son of Man who descends and ascends, the Light, prophet, and Messiah who was coming into the world, and the Word that became flesh). In this chapter we will focus, as others have, on what Jesus speaks about, which is largely about himself, but we will find that the use of

4

multiple identifiers and multiple conceptual systems has the same problematic effect of referent blurring synonymy that we saw in the prologue. Which means, too, that Jesus speaks the same language as the narrator, while all other characters speak everyday language, including Jesus' disciples, who did not learn the special language until after he was gone.[9] The chapter concludes with some observations about how John's Light system helps to explain both the semantic referent blurring of his special language and its contrastive style, including the social contrast between the "sons of Light" and those who "loved darkness."

The explanatory attempt with which Chapter 3 ends is at best incomplete, and therefore in Chapter 4 we will turn to the sociology of Light as it is represented in John's narrative. Here we will examine the relationships between "the disciples of Moses" and the disciples of Jesus who are, respectively, the lovers of darkness and the "sons of Light," between the "disciples of Moses" and Jesus, who *is* the Light, and between Jesus and Moses. We will find that the sons of Light have been rejected by the disciples of Moses in Jesus' time, just as they had rejected Jesus, but also in John's time, just as Jesus predicted. But more important, we will find that having become an outcast society by virtue of their having been rejected and killed by the leaders of the dominant Jewish society to which they had belonged, the sons of Light created an anti-language in order to legitimate for themselves their identity as an anti-society.[10] The notion of an anti-language helps us to solve the problem of why John used everyday language in a special way, for this anti-language is what we have been calling John's special language. What is special about it is not simply its difference from the everyday, but its opposition to the everyday. The critical factor in this anti-language proves to be the image of Moses maintained by his "disciples," for many of the key terms in John's characterization of Jesus are derived from key terms in the image of Moses against which John reacts. The anti-language is "anti-" because its terms are derived from the image and transformed in contrastive or anti-structural ways. For example, Moses is said to have ascended and descended, but Jesus first denies this and then *inverts* the order of verbs, claiming that *he* has descended and ascended; Moses is said to have seen God, but Jesus denies it and says that only the Son has seen God and made him known. And so on, and relentlessly so. As in the prologue, contrast, negation, and inversion prevail, and so does the referent blurring for, as we will find in Chapter 3, the multiple identifiers and conceptual systems come into play in what is affirmed about Jesus, the Word that became flesh, the Light that has come into the world, the only Son sent by the Father, and the Son of Man who descended. The notion of anti-language therefore also helps us to solve problems of both the form and the content of John's special language.

The anti-Moses aspect of John's special language helps us to solve yet another problem, namely the reason why John also characterized Jesus in terms of the feminine personification of the wisdom (Sophia) of God found in certain Jewish Wisdom texts. In Chapter 5 we will find that the image of Sophia known to John contributes as much to his characterization of Jesus as the image of Moses that he knew, while also providing the structure of his narrative's plot. The new perspective is that John turns to the image of Sophia because in some of its forms it already contains anti-Moses features that are congenial to John's purposes. For example, whereas Moses was sent to Israel from the mountain *with* the Law, Sophia was sent from heaven *as* the Law, thus displacing Moses. And like Jesus, some Wisdom texts both deny that anyone has ascended into heaven to bring wisdom to earth and claim that from heaven God gave Wisdom/Sophia to his beloved people. There is much more here, too, but the point is that John moved from the image of Moses in the Sophia system he knew to Sophia herself, and then he systematically displaced *her* with the Word and with Jesus. Like Sophia, the Word was with God from the beginning and was active in creation. Like Sophia, the Son was sent/given by God to Israel whom he loved, and like Sophia he "dwelt" among God's people, offering life to those who accepted him, while those who rejected him die. Like Sophia, the Son makes "friends" of God, and like Sophia, who is Light and has "children," Jesus, who is the incarnate Light, makes "friends" and engenders "sons of Light." And like Sophia, the Son speaks of himself, of whence he has come and why he has come, in the first-person singular. But John's Jesus is also anti-structurally unlike Sophia because of the anti-language he created in reaction to the image of Moses and to the social circumstances in which he encountered it. For while Sophia speaks everyday language, Jesus speaks John's special language, and while Sophia comes to dwell in Israel permanently as the Law and the source of life in the world, the Son returns to his primordial unity with the Father, and he will eventually bring his own with him because life in the world is death, a thing to be hated, even as the world hated him and his people.

That the world hated Jesus and his people is the perception from which John begins. But his narrative is also a response to this perception and to the social experience that generated it. His response is that God loved the world, and that by sending his Son he gave the world the possibility of life. Those who believe in the Son have this life, while those who do not believe die. However, the seemingly clear terms of this response—that God loved the world and sent his Son to give it life—are in fact terms drawn from John's special language, where 'God,' the 'world,' the 'Son,' and 'life' do not mean what they mean in the everyday use of language. What they mean in the special language is the subject of our initial concern with John's special language. Let us therefore turn to his own use of this language in the prologue to his truly remarkable narrative.

Chapter 1

The Narrator's Use of Language in John 1:1–18

The prologue to John's narrative is addressed directly to its audience by one who claims to be among those who beheld the glory of the incarnate Word, and received from him "grace upon grace" and "the power to become children of God" (1:12–18). These claims are therefore made in the language of a particular group of people, and this language is being used to represent that group's understanding of its experience. However, both the language and the experience are problematic. Although we can understand the individual words, which are drawn from everyday language, both in the original Greek and in the English translations the words do not mean or denote[1] what they do in everyday language because they are used to refer to things that are not part of everyday experience. In everyday experience and language, 'words' do not 'become flesh', they do not possess the property of 'glory', in the sense of either honor or luminosity,[2] and we do not 'behold' 'glory' in an incarnate 'Word', because in everyday terms that is an inconceivable event. For this reason, too, we do not know what is meant and referred to when the narrator says that he and others "received grace upon grace" from the "fullness" of the 'Word become flesh'. But the narrator's self-consciousness about his distinctive use of everyday language is made explicit when he defines what he means by 'becoming children of God' as being "born, not of blood nor of the will of the flesh nor of the will of man, but of God." Being 'born' does not mean what it normally means, and therefore we do not know what he is referring to when he talks about 'becoming children of God', of which he only tells us what it is *not*. So the narrator is using everyday language, but he is using it in a special way, a way that is both implicitly and explicitly contrasted with everyday usage. In this sense, we can say that he uses a special language, one that we will later call an anti-language because of its opposition to an everyday language which he presupposes—and even uses.[3] But this is to get ahead of ourselves. Our task now is to explore in greater detail some of the peculiarities of the narrator's use of language and some of the issues it raises.

The narrator's very first sentence (1:1) is often praised for its poetic beauty, yet it also represents the fundamental semantic problem in his use of language. The first two clauses reflect the everyday use of language to identify states, things, qualities, and relations by differentiating them: "In the beginning was the Word, and the Word was with God." Regardless of what the word "Word" means,[4] these two statements are linguistically comparable to saying "There is a boat, and the boat is on the water." The nouns denote different entities, the verbs assert that these entities exist(ed), and the prepositions identify a spatial relationship between them. However, the everyday use of language is violated by the third clause in the narrator's opening sentence: "and the Word was God." Here, the entities that language initially served to differentiate, and then to relate by spatial juxtaposition, are said to be identical: to say that the Word *is/was* God is comparable to saying that the boat *is* the water.[5] These assertions violate everyday language (and logic) because the nouns no longer serve to differentiate either meanings or entities. If the boat is said to *be* the water, then the words "boat" and "water" do not refer to different things and therefore, too, the words do not mean or denote what they do in everyday language. So, too, with John's use of language. The words 'Word' and 'God' cannot have their conventional meaning or denotation because they are used to refer to the same entity, which is neither of the entities they are usually used to refer to. Consequently, without further information (which the narrator does not provide), we can know neither the meaning of his words nor the referent of his statement. And this problem is only compounded by verse 2a, when the narrator reiterates verse 1b by saying again that the Word was "with God." The narrator doubly violates everyday language, first by using two words denoting different classes of things to refer to the same thing, and second by also using them to refer to different things. In terms of everyday language, what he says does not make sense and we cannot identify what he is referring to. Because he uses the words and grammar of everyday language, we can understand what he is *saying*, but we cannot understand what he *means* because we do not know to what he is *referring*.

From the first four clauses of John's narrative we can see that the critical issue posed by his special use of language is the problem of its reference. But we can also see that this problem is linguistically created by his using words as synonyms when they are not synonyms in everyday language.[6] And, logically, he is contradictory because he is predicating of two different things that they are both different and identical. For us to understand what John means, we would have to be able to identify the referents that would make his language meaningful. Clearly, however, John's language is a special language, one that is used to speak about a world (i.e., of referents) that is different from the everyday world that everyday language enables us to speak about. Whether or not the referents of his language *can* be identified is a problem we will have to wrestle with. But before we take on that task, let us explore a possible alternative to my reading of the narrator's opening statements.

It could be argued that my reading is overly literal and that it overlooks the possibility that John's language is 'symbolic' or 'metaphorical'. The notion of symbol, however, is not of much help because symbolic meaning also depends on knowing the referents of the symbols.[7] But the notion of metaphor is another matter, not only because John employs metaphors, but also because in one of its functions a metaphor can be used noncontradictorily to say that one thing is another. Let us take the following as a working definition of metaphor: *"Metaphor is that figure of speech whereby we speak about one thing in terms which are seen to be suggestive of another."*[8]

And let us also take as a case in point a classic example that sounds very much like John's "the Word was God": *The man is a lion.* The question is, are we to understand John's statement in the same metaphorical way that we understand the statement that a man is a lion? Taken literally, the assertion that a man is a lion is nonsense for all of the reasons I have given in arguing that John's statement does not make any sense either. Taken metaphorically, however, "the man is a lion" makes sense because we understand this statement to be saying that the man has lion-like qualities. The metaphorical use of 'lion' here attributes qualities associated with the referent of the word 'lion' to the referent of the word 'man.' Grammatically, therefore, we interpret the verb "is" as a predicative rather than an equative copula, and in so doing we understand the statement to be asserting not that a certain man *is* a lion but that he is lion-like.[9] In this light, to interpret "the Word was God" metaphorically, we would have to read the verb "was" as a predicative copula and understand the statement to mean that 'the Word was God-like'. Is this what John means?[10] I think not, for both before and after saying that "the Word was God" he posits the separate existence of the referents of both 'the Word' and 'God'. In *this* light, we would not construe metaphorically the statement "the man is a lion" if the speaker had also said, "there is a man, and there is a lion." But let us pursue the question of metaphor further, because asking whether a statement is to be construed literally or metaphorically can itself help us better to understand what makes John's use of language special.

In verse 5 the narrator says, "The light shines in the darkness and the darkness has not overcome [or did not receive] it,"[11] and in verse 9 he makes a parallel assertion that "the true light that enlightens every man was coming into the world; he was in the world . . . yet the world knew him not . . . and his own people received him not." Some critics think that John often uses the word 'light' metaphorically.[12] We will return to this idea shortly, but first let us reflect on just what is and what is not metaphorical in these two statements.

In and of itself, the statement "the light shines in the darkness and the darkness has not overcome it" need not be construed metaphorically. It is only when this statement is read along with the one in verse 9 that the possibility of metaphor arises. Light *shining in the darkness* could be a metaphor for light *coming into and being in the world*. 'Shining' could be a metaphor for 'coming into' and 'being in', while 'darkness' could be a metaphor for 'the world'. The world would be assigned the attribute of darkness, but would not *be* darkness, and 'coming into' and

11

'being in' would be given the attribute of shining without *being* shining. Thus far, we have a plausible case for metaphor, but if we go further matters become considerably more complicated. Problems begin when we see that 'light' is the subject of *both* statements. In the first one, 'light' seems to denote solar light, to which 'shining' and 'in the darkness' are conventionally appropriate. In the second one, however, 'light'[13] is anthropomorphized by such expressions as "coming into," "being in," "was made through him," "he came to his own home," and "his own people." What is the problem? The problem is that verse 5 is not a metaphor for verse 9, but vice versa; verse 9 is an anthropomorphic metaphor for the statement in verse 5. But this also means that 'light' is not a metaphor in either statement, although what is said about it in the metaphors of verse 9 must make us wonder if John has the everyday understanding of solar light in mind. Once again, let us delay pinning down just what John might intend with his use of the word 'light' in order to see how that word retains its connotation of luminosity. For in verse 9, the Greek word *photizei*, which is often translated by the psychologically subjective word 'enlightens', also has the conventional sense of 'illuminates', which corresponds better to the word "shines" in verse 5. To be sure, however, the narrator may very well be playing with the two senses of the Greek word, because 'enlightens' would be consistent with the rest of the anthropomorphizing in verse 9.[14] This possibility also exists with another word that John uses elsewhere with a clear play on meanings, the word *doxa*, which connotes both 'honor' and 'glory', and in the sense of 'glory' denotes the quality of luminosity, the radiance, for example, of the presence of Israel's God.[15] In verse 14, however, when the narrator speaks of having beheld the 'glory' of the Word after it had become flesh, luminosity is the more likely object of 'beholding' than is 'honor'. Thus the literal use of the notion of 'light' is extended by the words *photizei* and *doxa*.

We can now take up the question of just what the narrator is referring to when he speaks of 'light'. We have seen that he is not using the word metaphorically, but does this mean that he is using it literally, and if not, what *could* he be meaning and referring to?

Although the punctuation of verses 3–4 is problematic,

such that 'life' could be understood as residing either in the 'Word' or in what 'came into being',[16] two statements are clearly made. One is that "all things came into being through" the Word (v. 3), and the other is that "the life was the light of men" (v. 4b). Let us begin with the second statement.

Because John later says that Jesus was the Word, the Light, and the Life (e.g, 1:9–11, 14; 11:25; 14:6), verse 4 should probably be read as saying that 'Life', now capitalized, like 'Light' and 'the Word', was 'in the Word', and that "the Life was the Light of men." How are we to understand these assertions? On the face of it, they could be understood metaphorically as meaning that 'Life' and 'Light' are metaphors, respectively, for 'the Word' and 'the Life'. In this sense, the quality of life would be attributed to 'the Word', and the quality of light would be attributed to 'the Life'. But if this metaphorical reading is correct, we at least have a very peculiar *sequence* of predications, one in which the problem of reference remains. "The Word" would have to have literal reference to whatever John intends this expression to refer to, because it would be metaphorically granted the quality of life, which would now have to be uncapitalized. However, when we then read that "the Life was the Light of men," 'Life' would have to be capitalized and understood to refer literally, for the now uncapitalized 'light' would be a metaphorical attribute of 'the Life'. Consequently, "the Word" would refer literally, "the L/life" would refer *both* literally *and* metaphorically, and "the light" would only refer metaphorically. But is this the case? Are we in fact dealing with metaphors? I think not.

The alternative to a metaphorical reading is to interpret all three nouns as having literal reference. If 'the Word' and 'God' refer literally, so could 'the Life' and 'the Light', and we have already seen that in verses 5 and 9–11 'the Light' does refer literally. Viewed in this way, 'the Life' could be *"in"* the 'Word' just as 'the Word' was *"with"* God, and 'the Light' *being* "the Life of men" could be understood in terms of 'the Word' *being* God. However much this would violate the everyday use of language, 'the Word', 'God', 'the Life', and 'the Light' could all be used synonymously to refer literally to the same referential entity. That this is so can be seen by turning to the first statement we noted in verse 3.

The synonymity of 'the Word' and 'the Light' is established by the fact that in the prologue *creation* is predicated of both of them. In verse 3 it is predicated of 'the Word' (*panta di' autou egeneto*), and in verse 10 it is predicated of 'the Light' (*ho kosmos di' autou egeneto;* see v. 9 for 'Light' as the antecedent of the pronoun). Because the one creation of "all things"/"the world" is attributed to both 'the Word' and 'the Light', these latter two expressions are used synonymously to refer to the same referent. This conclusion, moreover, is confirmed by the further fact that Jesus is (implicitly) both 'the Word' in its incarnate form (1:14) and 'the Light' as it appeared in the world, went to his own home, and was rejected by his own people (1:9–11). What, then, of 'the Life'? If we interpret the verb "was" in verse 4 as an equative copula, 'the Life' is synonymous with 'the Light'. And as we have seen, this interpretation is supported by the fact that Jesus, who is 'the Word' and 'the Light', also claims to *be* 'the Life'.

Finally, there remains the question of the relationship between these three synonyms and the word 'God', which we have also seen to be used synonymously with 'the Word'. Because of this synonymity, the *four* expressions are synonymous, and what we concluded about the implications of the synonymity of 'the Word' and 'God' holds for all four of them. Their reference is literal, not metaphorical, and because they are each used to refer to the same entity, not the different ones that they denote in everyday language, none of them *means* what it means in everyday language and therefore we cannot know either what they mean or to what they refer. All that we can say of their reference is that for John there is an Other that is the originator of the world and that It subsequently entered into the world in the form of the human being Jesus of Nazareth. And because none of the words means or denotes what it does in everyday language, this Other is *not* the God referred to in that language. John uses the word 'God' differently, and he understands its denotation and referent differently, despite the fact that his Other is responsible for many of the same things (here, creation) that are attributed to the God of the everyday language. John redefines 'God', and one of the principal ways in which he does so is by his further insistence that the Other is not known in the world apart from Jesus (1:14, 18).

Thus far we have seen that Jesus is the Word become flesh

and the Light that has come/shines into/in the world. But there is another set of terms that the narrator employs to represent the relationship between the Other and Jesus, 'Father' and 'Son', or, as in 1:14 and 18, the 'only Son', which in the Greek is the single word *monogenes*, which denotes the 'only offspring'.[17] These terms introduce yet another aspect of John's special use of language.

Immediately after saying that "the Word became flesh and dwelt among us, full of grace and truth," the narrator asserts: "We have beheld his glory, glory as of the only Son from the Father, full of grace and truth" (v. 14). He continues by saying that "from his fullness have we received, grace upon grace" (v. 16), and that "grace and truth came through Jesus Christ" (v. 17b). And he concludes by stating that "no one has ever seen God; the only Son, who is in the bosom of the Father, he has made him known" (v. 18). There are a number of issues in these statements and others not quoted from 1:14–18 that we will deal with later. For now, let us focus on some issues posed by the quoted statements that are significant both for John's special use of language and for his characterization of Jesus.

First, it is important to recognize that a shift in the narrator's point of view takes place in 1:14–18.[18] In 1:1–13, his focus is on the Other and its relationship to the world, and his speech is in the third person; he is describing the activities of others. However, in 1:14–18 his speech is in the first person ("we" in vv. 14 and 16) and his point of view is that of people who beheld and received things from the incarnate Other, who is now and for the first time identified as "the only Son from the Father." With this shift in point of view, John ceases to talk about the Other independently of the 'Son' who makes the Other known as his 'Father'. 'Father' and 'Son' language is therefore everyday language that is here used to represent the relationship between the human being Jesus of Nazareth and the pre-incarnate Other, of which Jesus is said to be the incarnate form in the world. Prior to the incarnation of the Other, there is only the Other who is differentiated from the world, but after the incarnation there is the Other and Jesus, who is the form of the Other's presence in the world. In order to understand John's use of the everyday kinship language of 'Father' and 'Son', it is necessary to realize that the Other's entry into the world in the 'flesh' of Jesus is also

15

an entry into the language of the world, which is a language that, among other things, is designed to differentiate things by giving them different "names." Consequently, prior to the incarnation there is no differentiation in the Other, and therefore prior to that moment there is no 'Father' any more than there is a 'Son'. By the same token, 'Jesus' is not a pre-existent divine being who came into the world; it is the Other who came into the world by 'becoming flesh'. In this light, therefore, 'Father' and 'Son' are words from everyday language that are employed metaphorically to refer to the relationship between the Other and its incarnate form during the limited time of its incarnation.

The Other is not a literal 'father' any more than Jesus is its literal 'son'.[19] The metaphors are saying that their relationship during the period of the incarnation is something *like* the relationship between a father and his only son. Later in the narrative, John will also say that the Father 'sent' his Son, using the verb 'send' as a metaphor for a process that other language is also used to describe. We have already seen one set of such terms in the assertions that the Light "was coming into the world," (1:9–12), and it will be recalled that these terms are metaphorical predications of the Light's shining in the darkness. But these two metaphorical systems now raise the further question whether or not "the Word became flesh and dwelt among us" is also a metaphorical predication about the 'Word'. As we have seen, 'the Word' refers literally to the Other, and it is also the case that the word 'Jesus' refers literally to a certain man who bears this name. Literally, the clause is saying that 'the Word became Jesus'. But does this render "became flesh and dwelt among us" as metaphorical? No, it does not, for Jesus literally is a flesh-and-blood human being and he literally "dwelt among" fellow human beings. Like creation, the narrator understands the incarnation literally, although he never explains exactly how the Word 'became' Jesus, who had human parents (1:45; 2:3).

Strictly speaking, the language of 'father' and 'son' applies only to the time of the incarnation, and for this reason it belongs to the principal but not the sole semantic system used to represent the relationship between Jesus and the Other in the rest of the narrative.[20] However, there are times when the narrator and Jesus speak about the incarnate Other as the Son when talking about pre-incarnate and post-incarnate times, as in 1:18, where the narrator refers to the post-incarnate Son as now being in "the bosom of the Father." Similarly, in 17:5 and 24 the Son speaks about the pre-incarnate glory which he had with his Father before the world was created. How are we to understand such statements? John and Jesus are not referring to the human being Jesus as such, because prior to the incarnation the Other is undifferentiated in itself and because Jesus was born of human parents and in fact died. Therefore, when John speaks about the post-incarnate Son being "in the bosom of the Father," this is a metaphor—one among others—representing the re-union of the Other with itself. Father and Son language in these anomalous instances is employed by the narrator because his narrative point of view has been oriented to *Jesus* as 'the Son'. So, too, later locutions, such as the Son's 'returning to' or 'ascending to' the Father are also metaphors for the process of re-union, and they have their corresponding terms in the metaphors of the Son having been 'sent' and 'descending'. On the other hand, the notion of the Son's 'glorification' is probably a literal description of re-union because it occurs after Jesus' death and refers to the resumption of the 'glory' which existed before the foundation of the world.[21] So two things must be remembered about this Father and Son language. First, it applies solely to the time of the incarnation of the Other, and second, because of the narrator's orientation to the 'Son', he frequently employs it inappropriately to refer to pre- and post-incarnate times.

Verses 14–18 raise yet another issue concerning the relation of the Other to Jesus. "Glory" and "grace and truth" are said to have been "beheld" in the incarnate Other, Jesus, and "grace and truth" have been received by others from him. Because "the Word" is the antecedent of the pronoun "his" in "his glory," 'glory', at least in verse 14a, is a quality of "the Word." However, in verse 14b the word 'glory' is repeated in the expression, "glory as of the only Son from the Father." Accordingly, the 'glory' of 'the Word' is experienced in the flesh of Jesus, but as "the glory of the only Son from the Father." The question posed by this phrasing concerns the possibility that the word 'glory' is employed literally in the first clause, subject to the conditions of John's special language, and that it has the sense of luminosity noted earlier, while in the second clause it is employed metaphorically, with the sense of honor, as befitting an only son, which is a metaphorical use of kinship language. We will take up this question again in the next chapter when we consider John's play with so-called double meanings. Suffice it to say for now, however, that if this interpretation is correct, it would provide another instance of metaphor being necessitated by the notion of the incarnation of the Other, not only in 'flesh', but also in everyday language (see above on 1:9–11). But what, now, of "grace and truth"? Are these also metaphors, and if so, of what are they metaphors?

These are much more difficult questions to answer because neither these words nor related ones are used previously in the prologue. It would appear, however, that because the incarnate Other is said to be "full of grace and truth" and that others received these things from him, they are not personal qualities of Jesus but of the Word which became incarnate in him and, like the Word's glory, became manifest in him. However, to answer our questions, we have to turn to another aspect of John's special use of language in the prologue, one that is related to his play with synonymy.

Up to now, we have found that synonymy is associated with the Other, both in itself and in the processes of its 'coming into the world' and 'returning' whence it came. But we also find in the prologue cases of synonymy associated with the *reception* of what has 'come into the world', and in these cases we find another aspect of John's special use of language, its *contrastive* dimension. In verses 10–12, we find it said of the light that came into the world, that "the world knew [*egno*] him not" and "his own people received [*parelabon*] him not," but that some "received [*elabon*] him," and "believed [*pisteuousin*] in his name." The verb 'believe' is also found in verse 7b, a form of the verb 'receive' appears in verse 5 (*katelaben*), preceded by a negative "not," and a verb associated with 'knowing' occurs in verse 18 (*exegesato*). Clearly, the narrator has in mind three sets of contrastive terms, although he does not here employ each of the terms: receive/not receive; know/not know; believe/not believe. In the course of his narrative after the prologue, all of these terms are used, and from that usage as well as from his usage here, it is apparent that he employs each of these sets synonymously with each of the other sets. That is to say, 'receiving', 'knowing', and 'believing' are synonymous with each other, as are their negated forms.[22] What is more, the contrastive sets correspond to two contrasted social groups, those who 'received' the incarnate Other and those who did not, and the narrator is a representative of those who did. So there is a social corollary to the narrator's linguistic usage, a corollary to which we will return in subsequent chapters. Suffice it to say for now that if John's special use of language is an anti-language, as mentioned earlier, it is the language of an anti-society, one that is opposed to and by the society that did not "receive" the Light.

In addition to these sets of terms, we should further observe that in 1:14–18, 'beholding' (v. 14) and 'receiving' (v. 16) refer to actions related to the same grammatical objects, "grace and truth" (cf. v. 17), suggesting that these verbs are also used synonymously.[23] Similarly, because 'receiving' is used of both "grace and truth" (vv. 16–17) and "the Light" (v. 12, with the antecedent noun in v. 9), we must take seriously the possibility that these objects of 'receiving' are also synonymous, as are the several designations of the Other in 1:1–5. Indeed, because 'beholding' is also used of "the Word" (v. 14), which we have seen to be synonymous with "the Light," "grace and truth" would be synonymous with "the Word" as well as "the Light," and "grace" and "truth" should be capitalized, as "truth" should be capitalized later, when Jesus claims to be "the Truth" (14:6).[24] And this synonymity answers the questions we asked earlier about whether or not "grace" and "truth" are metaphors. They are not, because they are further synonyms for the Other. Indeed, Jesus is said to have come "to bear witness to the Truth" (18:17) just as John the Baptist is said to have come "to bear witness to the Light" (1:8).

The notion of 'light' leads us to another significant contrast that we have already looked at, namely the contrast between 'Light' and 'darkness' in 1:5. Because the narrator uses the word 'world' literally, although with the nuance of 'social world',[25] and because we have found verse 5 to be literally intended, 'darkness' is a synonym for 'the world'.[26] What is of particular interest in the present context is that later in the narrative John contrasts those who "*come to* the Light" with those who "*walk in* darkness," and in the process renders these expressions synonymous with the synonyms associated with the contrast between 'receiving' and 'not receiving' (3:17–21; 8:12; 12:35–36, 46). In fact, in 12:36 'believing in the Light' makes it possible to become "sons of Light," which appears to be a metaphorical synonym for the metaphor of 'becoming children of God' in 1:12–13.[27] And thus, too, the contrast between 'Light' and 'darkness' provides the basis for the title of this study, *The Sociology of Light*, which is also the title of Chapter 4.

Before we entertain a final example of John's contrastive style, we should be aware that the contrasts between synonymous sets of terms having to do with 'receiving' and 'not receiving' have the same effect as the synonyms used to refer to the Other. On the one hand, 'receiving' does not mean receiving as of an object, 'knowing' does not mean knowing some particular information or object, and 'believing' does not mean believing that something is true or false. And 'beholding' is not 'observing', because only some people 'beheld' the 'glory' of 'the Word' in Jesus. Jesus did not have something like a halo that all could observe. On the other hand, because of the synonymity of these words, which obscures their everyday meaning and denotation, we do not know to what they are referring. As a result, John's special use of language obscures the referents of the two most critical objects of his discourse, the Other and the nature of the experience that is represented in 'receiving' and its synonyms.[28] And related to these is the further obscurity of the process by which the Other became Jesus, for it, too, is blurred by the multiple synonyms of 'shining' and 'becoming flesh', to which we will have to add yet others when we consider such notions as the Son having been 'sent' and the Son of Man having 'descended'.[29] Synonymy is therefore one of the distinctive features of John's special language. But there remains another feature that is related to his contrastive style.

Thus far, we have been concentrating on the dictionary of John's special language and, in addition to his creation of synonyms, we have found that his word selection is frequently a matter of establishing contrasts between terms. However, his contrasting terms are rarely semantic opposites or antonyms,[30] such as 'light' and 'darkness'. Rather, and distinctively, he creates negative opposites either by grammatically negating the positive term or expression, as in his contrast between 'receiving' and '*not* receiving', or by following a negative statement with an adversative ("but") clause that expresses a positive statement. The number of such negations in 1:1–18 is quite remarkable: "All things were made through him, and without him was *not* anything made" (v. 3); "The Light shines in the darkness, and the darkness has *not* overcome it" (v. 5); "He was *not* the Light, *but* came to bear witness to the Light" (v. 8; "The true Light" in v. 9 functions like an adversatively positive contrast with "he was not the Light"); "the world was made through him, and the world knew him *not*" (v. 10); "he came to his own home, and his own people received him *not*" (v. 11); "*but* to all who received him, . . ." (v. 12); "who were born, *not* of blood *nor* of the will of the flesh *nor* of the will of man, *but* of God" (v. 13); "we have beheld" (v. 14) continues the adversatively positive contrasts with the negative statements in 1:10–11; "*No one* has ever seen God; the only Son . . . has made him known" (v. 18). In addition to the grammatically marked contrasts, there are at least two, and probably three others. In 1:15 the Baptist says that Jesus "ranks" before him.[31] In 1:17, there is an implicit contrast between the Law that came through Moses and the "Grace and Truth" that came through Jesus. And it is probable that the phrase "no one has ever seen God" in verse 18 is an implicit negation of a claim that Moses *had* seen God.[32] From all of these instances, it is evident that contrasts pervade the narrator's thinking as well as his use of language.[33]

To conclude our study of the narrator's use of language in 1:1–18, we cannot help but acknowledge that his usage stands in fundamental contrast to everyday usage. John and his people speak and think in ways that are in contrast with the speech and thought of others in their social environment. These others, moreover, are as it were the lords of the everyday, of the conventional and of the traditional. They are the maintainers of norms to which John and his people oppose themselves, linguistically, conceptually, and, not least of all, socially. We cannot appreciate John's special use of language without acknowledging its social function as an affirmation of difference over against the sameness of the world around him and his people, a world that has also rejected what they affirm. Indeed, we will find that the fact of social rejection is the motivating force behind the affirmation of a difference that has been imposed upon John and his people.[34]

In terms of the narrator's use of language in the prologue to his narrative, difference is represented both by his creation of synonyms out of words that in everyday language are not synonyms and by his relentless use of contrastive expressions. And we have found that synonymy raises the fundamental conceptual problem of the *reference* of his special use of language. Because his use of language renders it opaque to what he is referring to, we will not come to understand him better by seeking the referents of his language. Any better understanding we might obtain will come not from reference but from *difference*. In the prologue to his narrative, difference has been signaled by his deviations from everyday language. Beginning in our next chapter difference will be found in the different ways that different actors speak. Their use of language is a distinctive feature in John's system of characterization, for Jesus speaks the language that the narrator speaks and all other actors speak in everyday terms. As a result, Jesus and others are usually at conceptual odds with one another, and this contributes to the plot of the narrative because the way in which Jesus is understood by others leads to his arrest and death.

Chapter 2

Language and Characterization 1: How Jesus Speaks

As we have seen in our study of the narrator's prologue, language has both 'how' and 'what' aspects, in the sense that the use of language entails both how one speaks and what one speaks about. In this and the next chapter, our concern will be with the ways in which language is used in the construction of characters such as Jesus, his disciples, and others. In this chapter we will focus on how Jesus and others speak, and on the consequences and implications of their linguistic encounters. In the next chapter, we will focus on what Jesus speaks about. These are only foci, however, for the 'how' and the 'what' are not always easy to separate.

Following his prologue, in which he tells the reader a number of things about the Other and Jesus, the narrator begins to tell a sequence of stories about encounters between various characters, all of whom are native speakers of everyday language. For the most part, the narrator satisfies himself with using everyday language to describe these encounters, and he reserves the use of his special language for Jesus' speech to other characters, all of whom know only the everyday language, including Jesus' disciples who in his time did not speak the special language. Otherwise, we only see the narrator's hand in the often peculiar construction of individual episodes. In order for us to see how the narrator plays with the use of language, it is best to follow his discourse story by story for a few chapters, in commentary fashion. Then, once we have gained a sense of what he is doing, we will turn to some more general observations without regard for narrative sequence.

1:19–28

The very first episode in 1:19–28 comes as somewhat of a linguistic jolt after the obscurities of the prologue. Although the narrator links this episode to the prologue by developing the theme of the Baptist's testimony referred to in 1:6–8 and 15, the language of both the Baptist and his Jewish questioners is classically everyday.[1] Jews have seen him baptizing and conclude that he must be either "the Christ," or "Elijah," or "the prophet," and therefore they ask which one he is. In addition to the everydayness of the language, the question about who John is presupposes everyday assumptions that someone who baptized had to be one of the three characters named. The Baptist's responses, on the other hand, are only marginally of the special language sort. He denies that he is any one of the three and claims to be the "one crying in the wilderness," of whom the prophet Isaiah spoke. Here the Baptist is playing the everyday game by saying that he is this, but not that, and he presumes that the "priests and Levites" questioning him understand his reference to Isaiah. The only traces of special language come in verse 20, where the narrator says that the Baptist responded to the question as to who he was by 'confessing' that he is "*not* the Christ." The narrator's insistence that John did not deny being the Christ, but confessed it, is related to the narrator's earlier statement that the Baptist came "for testimony, to bear witness to the Light" (v. 7), and the Baptist's saying that he is "*not* the Christ" is an echo of the narrator's statement, "he was *not* the Light" (v. 8). So while the Baptist and his interlocutors were communicating in everyday language, the narrator has also sent his readers a special language message in which the expression "the Christ" identifies Jesus as "the Light" in its worldly manifestation, although it is not clear that this is what the Baptist meant by "the Christ," for his meaning seems to be that of his interlocutors. But more of this shortly. Here, as later, we have to remember that while the characters in any given episode usually know only the information communicated in it, the reader knows the information given in the prologue and understands individual episodes accordingly.

24

The narrator's hand is also evident in the unusual beginning of his first episode, when in response to the question "Who are you?" the Baptist says that he is *not* "the Christ" before his interlocutors ask if he was the Christ. That is to say, the Baptist's response is not motivated by anything in the episode itself. His response is rather determined by the narrator's concern to link it to what *he* has said in his prologue. Equally unmotivated by the interlocutor's questions is John's response to the question of why he is baptizing if he is none of the three figures they named. He seems to be answering the question when he says that he is baptizing with water, but then he refers to something unrelated to the question, saying that someone stands among them whom they do not know, the one who "comes after him" and is superior to him (vv. 26–27). This is clearly a reiteration of testimony the narrator attributed to the Baptist in 1:15, but because it has nothing to do with the question he was asked, it must be understood as the narrator's showing the reader that John said what the narrator had already attributed to him. And this appears to be confirmed by the narrator's omission of any response by the Baptist's interlocutors. The narrator is not concerned about their response, and they cannot know what he is talking about, because only the reader has clues to his meaning from the narrator's prologue. The episode itself ends inconclusively with the narrator's unmotivated report as to where the event took place (v. 28).

1:29–34

That the narrator is more interested in the Baptist's answers than in the questions asked by the Jewish authorities, or in their response to the answers they received, is further indicated by the next episode, in verses 29–34, which is set on another day and in which the Baptist's speech has no internal audience. The narrator is here indirectly addressing *his* audience, just as he was in the opening episode. Here, the Baptist repeats the words the narrator attributed to him in 1:15 (v. 30), and then indirectly explains his earlier words about baptizing with water by contrasting this with Jesus' baptizing with "the Holy Spirit" (vv. 31, 33). Although the logic is obscure, the Baptist says that he baptized with water so that Jesus "might be revealed to Israel" (v. 31b). Whatever the logic may be, however, it is clear that the purpose of the narrator is to show that John admitted his inferiority to Jesus and bore witness to him, even though he had not known him previously. Curiously, the Baptist's 'witness' is also unmotivated within the episode. He knows that Jesus will baptize with the Holy Spirit because he had been given a sign to that effect (vv. 32–33), but there is no stated basis for his testimony that Jesus is "the Lamb of God, who takes away the sin of the world" (v. 29), or that he is "the Son of God" (v. 34). Nevertheless, with this testimony the narrator introduces two more 'names' for Jesus. "Son of God" resonates with "the only Son from the Father" in the prologue, and "Lamb of God" appears to be derived from the Greek translation of Isa. 53:12, where the word *pais*, which denotes both 'servant' and 'son,' is used of one who is said to have borne "the sin of many." "Lamb" would therefore be a substitute for and a synonym of "Son." Synonym or not, the three expressions, "only Son," "Son of God," and "Lamb of God," all *refer* to Jesus, and because of what we have seen of the reference of the narrator's special language we might suspect that they are being used synonymously. But yet other 'names' are given to Jesus in the next episodes, and those both raise some problems about the names the Baptist attributes to Jesus and clarify the suspected synonymy.

1:35–42

Naming is one way of constructing characters,[2] and the narrator introduces names for precisely this purpose. In 1:35–42 he has the Baptist identify Jesus as "the Lamb of God" to two of his disciples (v. 36), they address Jesus as "Rabbi," which the narrator says means "Teacher," translating from Aramaic to Greek (v. 38), and one of them, Andrew, tells his brother Simon that he has found "the Messiah," which the narrator says means "Christ," again translating from Aramaic into Greek (v. 41).[3] And Jesus gives Simon a new name, the Aramaic "Cephas," which the narrator yet again translates into Greek as meaning "Rock," although it is also treated as the proper name "Peter" (1:40, 44). What is most curious compositionally is that while the Baptist identifies Jesus as "the Lamb," and the two disciples address him with the honorific term "Rabbi,"[4] they also identify him as "the Messiah." Unless this is another example of unmotivated speech, the disciples would have had to have understood

26

"the Lamb" to denote "the Messiah." Either way, however, "the Messiah" and "Christ" are two more 'names' attributed to Jesus, although the reader already knows from the prologue (v. 8) and from the Baptist's "I am not the Christ" (v. 20) that *Jesus* is "the Christ," whatever, for the moment, the narrator may mean by that identification.

Three further points should be made about this episode. It marks the transition from the Baptist to Jesus, because John's disciples leave him to follow Jesus and because Jesus is henceforth the central actor. Jesus does not say much, but what he does say is in everyday language (vv. 38–39: "What do you seek?"; "Come and see"; and his renaming of Simon in v. 42). And last, we have both another example of apparently unmotivated speech, when Jesus says to Simon, "You are Simon the son of John," and another inconclusive episode, for no one responds to Jesus' renaming of Simon. Of these, Jesus' unmotivated speech may be less than innocent, as we can see in the next episode.

1:43–51

The story in 1:43–51 has some significant formal and material similarities to part of the preceding episode. In both cases, someone (Andrew, Philip) "finds" someone else (Peter, Nathanael) and tells him "we have found" Jesus ("the Messiah," "Jesus of Nazareth, the son of Joseph," "of whom Moses in the Law and also the prophets wrote"), and then Jesus identifies the first person who was found without having any apparent reason for knowing what he does about that person (the names of Simon and his father, and that Nathanael is a true Israelite "in whom is no guile").[5] The significance of this formal parallelism is that its corresponding parallelism of content adds to the characterization of Jesus, especially in what Andrew and Philip say about him, but also in the response that Nathanael makes but Peter did not. For after Jesus tells Nathanael that he is a true and guileless Israelite, Nathanael responds, "How do you know me?" (v. 48), to which Jesus answers that he "saw" him (he "looked at" Peter, v. 42) when he was under the fig tree, whereupon Nathanael says, "Rabbi, you are the Son of God! You are the King of Israel!" Jesus then counters by asking him, "Because I said to you, 'I saw you under the fig tree', do you believe?"

(v. 50a). Let us reflect on this bit of dialogue before we attend to what Andrew, Philip, and Nathanael say about Jesus.

In the episode involving Andrew, Simon, and Jesus, we found that Jesus' identification of Simon and his father was unmotivated; there was no reason for Jesus to know what he did. And we also noted that Simon did not ask Jesus how he knew who he was. In the story about Philip, Nathanael, and Jesus, however, motivation comes self-consciously into the foreground, both when Nathanael asks how Jesus knew who he was, and when Jesus answers with an explanation which on the face of it is not an explanation of how Jesus knew what he did, but only that he had "seen" Nathanael. Moreover, when Jesus asks Nathanael if his explanation was sufficient to make him "believe," Jesus, too, is drawing attention to the problem of motivation. Nathanael, construing things in everyday terms, interprets Jesus' knowledge about him as a wonder—he wondered how Jesus knew this, not only before receiving an explanation, but also afterward, because he concluded from what Jesus said that he must be "the Son of God" and "King of Israel." His implied reasoning is therefore very much like that of the Jewish authorities who saw John baptizing and concluded that he must be the Messiah, Elijah, or the prophet. Similarly, Jesus' final response to Nathanael is very much like John's response to the authorities. John admits to baptizing but points to something greater than that (vv. 26–27), and Jesus admits to how he knew who Nathanael was but also points to something greater: "You shall see greater things than these . . . You will see heaven opened, and the angels of God ascending and descending upon the Son of Man" (vv. 50b–51). The problem of motivation that we have observed in all of the episodes thus far is therefore not a matter of incompetent narrative style, but it is bound up with the contrast between motivation as construed in everyday terms and an *other* kind of motivation, one that does not make sense in everyday terms and, in everyday terms, can only be experienced as a wonder. And it *is* wondrous because, like all of the referent obscuring language seen in the prologue, the source of Jesus' knowledge is also obscured by the narrator.

The contrast between everyday understandings of what Jesus said and did and the understanding the narrator favors, however obscure it may be, is also represented in the understandings the narrator attributes to the Baptist, Andrew, Philip, and Nathanael. The Baptist identifies Jesus as "the Lamb of God" and "the Son of God"; Andrew identifies him as "the Messiah"/"Christ"; Philip knows him as "Jesus of Nazareth, the son of Joseph," but identifies him as "him of whom Moses in the Law and also the prophets wrote"; and Nathanael, who is at first dubious about anything good coming out of Nazareth, like the Baptist identifies him as "the Son of God," which he understands to be synonymous with "the King of Israel." It appears, therefore, that the identifications offered by the Baptist, Andrew, and Nathanael are synonymous with one another. But are they synonymous with 'the only Son'?

In this regard, Philip's identifications are especially significant. On the one hand, Philip's knowledge that Jesus is from Nazareth, and that he is the son of Joseph, is represented as common knowledge about Jesus. Jesus is known to be a human being, with a human father and a known place of origin in the world. From this we learn that the narrator understands the one in whom the Other became incarnate to have had a prior human biography; the Other became incarnate in an already existing human being.[6] However, because only the reader knows from the prologue that the incarnate Other is the "only Son from the Father," the everyday understanding the characters in the story have of him being the son of Joseph is only half correct, and in this case the 'half' is about as incongruous as being half pregnant. Without understanding that the son of Joseph *is* the "only Son from the Father," he is understood wrongly. And we will find that the narrator persistently plays with this misunderstanding.[7] But because Jesus is "the only Son from the Father," it is also the case that to understand him as "the Son of God" in the sense of "the King of Israel," as Nathanael does, is equally half correct and therefore equally totally wrong. When at the end of the narrative Jesus says that his "kingship is not of this world" (18:36), he totally undercuts the everyday meaning and denotation of the word 'king'. But if Nathanael's identifications are rendered suspect by 1:14, so also are all of the other identifications offered by the Baptist, Andrew, and Philip. Thus, and once again, the narrator's prologue gives the reader a perspective on individual episodes which the actors in them, apart from Jesus, do not have. Throughout the narrative, the reader is

29

required to employ the privileged knowledge given by the narrator while reading stories about characters who do not have this knowledge. The characters know and understand things in one way, and the reader understands them in another way. Indeed, the plot of the total narrative hinges on how characters act on the basis of the imperfect and therefore incorrect knowledge that they have.

Philip's now problematic identification of Jesus as the one about whom Moses and the prophets wrote requires further consideration. Clearly, he does not mean that they wrote about Jesus as being the son of Joseph and from Nazareth. Judging from 7:40–52, what they, here cited as "the scripture" (but see "the Law" in 7:49), wrote about was "the prophet" or "the Christ" and where "the Christ" comes from, which is reflected in Nathanael's question about anything good coming out of Nazareth. But this understanding of what Moses and the prophets wrote about is also subject to the problem of the only Son having come from the Father. It is one of the misunderstandings I just referred to. However, there is more to the problem than this, because later Jesus himself declares that "the scriptures . . . bear witness to" him and that Moses "wrote" about him (5:39, 46). In the context of this declaration, Jesus refers to both the Baptist and Moses ("the scripture") as bearing witness to him (5:31–36), and he does so in terms that reflect both the testimony and subordination to him that are expressed in the prologue (1:7–8, 15, 17).[8] How are we to understand what the narrator intends by affirming that Moses wrote about Jesus?

Because chapter 7 refers to "the prophet" and to where the Messiah "comes from," and because the narrative also reflects the notion of a "prophet who is to come into the world" and implicitly associates him with Moses (6:14), it is probable that the narrator and Philip are affirming that Jesus is the prophet who would come after Moses, as announced in the fifth book of the Law of Moses, in Deut. 18:15, 18.[9] However, as we can see from 6:25–51, the narrator and his character Jesus dispute Jewish interpretations of Moses while affirming what "Moses" himself wrote. In this light, the narrator is affirming that Moses wrote about "Jesus" but not what people thinking in everyday terms understood about what they read. And this also appears to be what the narrator intends when he says that the prophet Isaiah saw Jesus' glory and wrote about him, but that people in Jesus' time still did not believe in Jesus because their eyes had been blinded and their hearts hardened (12:36b–41). The question remains, however, as to what Philip understood by his statement. To answer the question, we have to examine Jesus' final words to Nathanael.

In 1:50–51 we receive the first intimation that Jesus' speech, here, what he speaks about, is different from everyday speech because it is far from clear as to what he is referring to. The problems arise in connection with the notions of 'seeing' and 'believing', which in the prologue were found to belong to the narrator's special language. Nathanael "saw" (vv. 46, 50) Jesus wondrously identify him, and he "believed" (v. 50), acknowledging him to be "the Son of God" and "the King of Israel." Nathanael's literal 'seeing' led him 'to believe' that Jesus was "the Son of God," and here 'seeing' and 'believing' are used in their everyday sense. Jesus seems to acknowledge that Nathanael 'believed', but when he speaks about greater things that will be seen in connection with him, he suggests that Nathanael's 'belief' is of a different sort from what *he* means by 'belief'. In addition, when Jesus refers to seeing "the heaven opened, and the angels of God ascending and descending upon the Son of Man," he appears to be contrasting the seeing of heavenly things with the seeing of earthly things, as he openly does later (cf. 3:12, 31–32). So Nathanael's 'belief' is presumably deficient because what he has 'seen' is inferior to what will be 'seen '. He has seen "the Son of Man," which in John refers to Jesus, but he has not yet seen the heavenly events of which Jesus speaks, cryptically alluding to the story of Jacob's ladder in Gen. 28:12. On the face of it, the meaning of this allusion is obscure, but a comparison of Jesus' statement with Genesis suggests a startling possibility.

In the story of Jacob, angels ascend and descend on a ladder that was set on the earth and reached to heaven. In Jesus' statement, his initial reference to heaven being opened implies that angels will descend from heaven and then ascend to heaven. But Jesus retains Genesis' sequence of ascending and descending and then substitutes the "Son of Man" for Jacob's "ladder." Implicitly, therefore, Jesus identifies himself as the ladder between the earth and heaven that makes traffic between them possible. This may sound farfetched,[10] but it is only another way of saying what Jesus says in 14:6: "I am the Way, and the Truth, and the Life; no one comes to the Father, but by me." It is therefore most likely that what seems to be everyday language in 1:51 contains a special language message, one whose referent is obscured because the implied identification of Jesus with the ladder between heaven and earth is but one of several synonymous expressions employed to represent an aspect of Jesus' relationship to heaven and earth. He is the means by which traffic between the two is possible.[11]

Finally, and with respect to Philip's understanding of the notion that Moses wrote about Jesus, because the book of Genesis is the first book of the Law attributed to Moses, Jesus' implicit identification of himself with Jacob's ladder would be an implied confirmation of Philip's claim at the beginning of the episode: Moses *did* write about Jesus in the Law. But because there is no indication that Philip had any more than the conventional understanding of the coming of a prophet like Moses, it is most improbable that he had the narrator's understanding of *how* Moses wrote about Jesus. However, what is true of Philip's statement is true of all of the identifications supplied by the Baptist, Andrew, and Nathanael: they had the right words but lacked the knowledge of their special language reference. The next story represents the same problem in a different but related way and in the process sheds more light on the problem.

2:1–11

'Seeing' and 'believing' are also involved in 2:1–11, the story of the wedding at Cana, where Jesus' deeds are more at issue than his words. His words are only significant because he angrily addresses his mother (cf. his brothers in v. 12) and says "My hour has not yet come" (2:4). What this 'hour' refers to is not explained here, but later we find that it refers to Jesus' 'glorification', which is 'his' return to the glory that he had "before the world was made" (17:5, 24). As we saw in our study of the prologue, 'glorification' denotes the reverse process of the Word's becoming incarnate, the Other's resumption of its pre-incarnation state. And this connection with the prologue is in fact made by the narrator at the conclusion of this episode, when he says that what Jesus did at Cana was "the first of his signs" in which "he manifested his glory" (2:11). But let us first look at the story of what Jesus did, for his deeds function like his special language words.[12]

Jesus, his mother, and his disciples are at a wedding feast where, when the wine runs out, his mother tells him about it and then instructs the servants to do whatever he says. He has them pour water into jars and then take some to the steward of the feast, who finds it to be wine but does not, like the servants, know where it came from. Consequently, he praises the bridegroom for having saved the good wine until the end of the celebration. And here the story ends, followed only by the narrator's comment to the reader, which may now be quoted in full: "This, the first of his signs, Jesus did at Cana in Galilee, and manifested his glory; and his disciples believed in him" (2:11).

Without the narrator's concluding comment, the story would only illustrate the steward's ignorance of where the wine came from. Nothing is said of what the servants understood about the transmutation of water into wine, nor of the bridegroom's response to the steward. Only the reader knows what the servants know, and it is to the reader that the narrator addresses himself in his conclusion. For the reader, there is a certain irony in the steward's mistaken notion that the bridegroom had saved the *best* wine until last, because the reader knows that *Jesus* produced this wine.[13] But an even greater irony comes to the fore in the narrator's conclusion, and this one is at the heart of his characterization of Jesus and of the plot of his narrative as a whole. For he who is known to all other actors as "Jesus of Nazareth, the son of Joseph," and whose mother and brothers are known as well, is known by the reader to be "the only Son from the Father." It is to this knowledge that the narrator appeals in his conclusion. His reference to Jesus manifesting his "glory" recalls for the reader the narrator's earlier claim that he and others "beheld" the glory of the Word in Jesus, "glory as of the only Son from the Father" (1:14). Within the story, the irony is that while the disciples and the other actors 'saw' what Jesus did, his disciples 'saw' what he did as a "sign" manifesting his "glory" and "believed in him," whereas it is implied that the others did not 'see' the sign or the glory and hence did not 'believe'. But what did the disciples believe? According to 1:14, they would have had to have believed that Jesus was the only

Son from the Father (cf. 1:12, "believed in his name"). As we have seen, however, this is different from Nathanael's 'belief' that Jesus was "the Son of God"/"King of Israel," and also from both the Baptist's and the disciples' earlier identification of Jesus as "the Lamb of God" and as "the Messiah/Christ." Is the narrator saying in 2:11 that for the first time the disciples saw a 'sign' and therefore 'believed' in a special language sense? This question calls for further reflection, on 'seeing', 'understanding', 'believing', and 'signs'.

The stories about Nathanael and about the wedding at Cana represent two different understandings of 'seeing' and 'believing'. We found in the story about Nathanael that what he saw was of such a nature as to diminish the value of the belief he professed. In effect, he 'saw' Jesus wondrously identify him and construed it as a sign indicating that Jesus was "the Son of God," just as others saw the Baptist baptizing and construed it as a sign that he was the Messiah, Elijah, or the prophet. This is the conventional or everyday understanding of signs, and it is found later in the narrative, when others see Jesus wondrously feed five thousand people and construe it as a sign that Jesus "is the prophet who is to come into the world" (6:14), in fulfillment of Moses' prediction in Deuteronomy 18. That is to say, they saw what Jesus did, understood it in terms of their knowledge about Moses' prediction, read the act as a sign, and believed that Jesus was the predicted prophet like Moses. Similarly, shortly after that episode, other people asked Jesus what sign he would do, "that we may see and believe you?," and then they cite the precedent of the mannah that Moses provided to his people in the context of the exodus from Egypt (6:30–31). These two examples therefore link the conventional notion of signs to Moses. Indeed, we cannot understand either this everyday notion of 'sign' or the narrator's special language understanding without appreciating the role of traditions surrounding Moses, which the narrator understands in one way and the actors in his narrative, apart from Jesus, understand in another.[14]

The conventional understanding of 'signs' derives especially from the story about God's sending Moses to deliver his people from Egypt. In Exodus 3–4, God tells Moses that he is sending him to deliver the people and that he is giving him a "sign" that he has been sent (3:10–12). In this story, there are two different kinds of signs, but their function is the same, namely to prove that Moses has been sent.[15] In Exod. 3:16–20 and 4:1–9, God tells Moses to inform the elders of Israel that he has appeared to him and given him a message for them. Moses responds that the elders will not believe what he says about God appearing to him, and God then provides him with three wonders that will be for the elders signs that what Moses told them was true; the sign will make them believe him. Moses' signs are therefore intended to engender belief in what he has said and lead to submission to what he says must be done. Needless to say, for those who later expected the arrival of a prophet like Moses, the performance of Moses-like signs would signify that the performer *was* the predicted one. And this is what we find in the conventional understanding of signs that we have seen in John. What, then, of John's special understanding of signs?

In John 6, the mannah provided in the wilderness is understood by "Jews" as a sign performed by Moses, and those who understand it as such expect as much from Jesus before they will believe what he says. However, according to Jesus, it is not Moses who provided the "bread from heaven," but Jesus' "Father," and he "gives," with an important use of the present tense, "the true bread from heaven" (6:31–33), and this 'bread' is *Jesus himself*: "I am the bread of Life" which has 'come down from heaven' and gives life to the whole world, not just to Israel (6:35, 38, 48–51b). Here, the conventional notion of sign as an act performed by someone to prove something else is replaced by the notion that Jesus *himself* is the sign.[16] To be sure, elsewhere Jesus performs acts that he as well as others construe as signs in the conventional sense, as in the feeding of the five thousand (see further, below). In the wedding at Cana, however, the servants who know that Jesus was responsible for transmuting water into wine are not represented as construing that act as a sign. Rather, the narrator says that only disciples saw the sign, and that they saw it as a manifestation of Jesus' "glory" (2:11). In the words of 1:14, they 'beheld the glory of the Word' in Jesus, "glory as of the only son from the Father." For the narrator, therefore, Jesus *is* the sign of the Father, and those who (really) see him see the Father, and those who (really) know him know the Father (14:7–11). Those who believe in Jesus do not believe in him, but in him who sent him. And those who see him see him who sent him (12:41–45).

In this sense, Jesus' acts are not simply signs pointing to something else, such as the believability of his words, but they are manifestations of his identity as the incarnate Other. Those who behold Jesus, in John's special language sense of the words 'behold', 'see', 'know', and 'receive', 'behold' the Other. And this is quite clearly not what is denoted by these verbs in everyday language, and neither is there any idea of sensory perception leading to language and meanings that make understanding in everyday terms possible, as among the people in John's narrative who 'see' X, 'think' Y, and 'believe' Z. In John's special language, these words do not mean what they mean in everyday language, and the everyday experience that they frame is not the experience to which John is referring. What it *is,* on the other hand, is not comprehensible, not only because John does not attempt to pin it down referentially, but also because he does not represent it as 'something', but as '*not* something'. As usual, however, John makes even this conclusion more complicated, and in doing so reopens the question whether the disciples' 'belief' at Cana was of this sort or of the conventional variety.

Complications arise from statements like that in 14:11, when Jesus says, "Believe me that I am in the Father and the Father in me; *or else believe me for the sake of the works themselves.*" Here, Jesus not only distinguishes between the two kinds of belief, but he also accepts both of them, thereby suggesting that however deficient Nathanael's belief was, it was still acceptable, and such is the case in a number of other instances in the narrative (cf. 4:19, 39–42, 48–54; 5:36; 7:31; 9 *passim;* 10:37–38; 12:37; 14:11; 20:28–29, and perhaps 20:30–31). The same point is made in a more complicated way in 10:37–38: "If I am not doing the works of my Father, then do not believe me; but if I do them, *even though you do not believe me, believe the works, that you may know and understand that the Father is in me and I am in the Father.*" As incredible as it may be, in this statement conventional belief in the signs on the one hand does *not* entail belief in what Jesus says, and on the other hand leads to 'knowledge' associated

36

with John's special understanding of 'belief'. 'Belief' in the works themselves is distinguished from 'believing' in Jesus, and the works themselves are sufficient to enable people to 'know' and 'understand' the unity of the Father and Jesus that is otherwise directly 'beheld' in the special notion of 'seeing' and 'believing'. As in the prologue, the narrator establishes differences and then equates what he has differentiated, leaving us in the dark as to what he is referring to. And for this reason we cannot answer the question we have been wrestling with concerning the relationship between the disciples' 'belief' at Cana and Nathanael's 'belief'. What is said of Jesus' deeds remains as enigmatic as what is reported of his speech.[17] Just as the incarnation reduces the Other to the sameness of humankind, the special use of language required to speak about the incarnation reduces the Other to the sameness of everyday language and the conventional thinking that language makes possible. Whether or not there are degrees of communicability through word and deed remains a question, but one thing is clear: The Other is only accessible in the human form of Jesus and in the human language and understanding that is a universal condition of human existence.[18] 'Belief' and its special language synonyms represent the apprehension of the Other, but we can no more explain this apprehension than we can explain the Other or the process of its 'becoming flesh'. And this is as true of the post-incarnation reports of the incarnational presence as it was, according to John, in the time of the incarnation. According to John, the same 'belief' that was possible in the time of the incarnation is possible for those who hear about it later (17:20; 20:29, 30–31). In the time of Jesus, the "Word became flesh," but afterwards the Word became *words*. Given this condition, we can only return to the narrative and explore further some other linguistic issues.

2:13–22

The episode in 2:13–22 consists of a story that the narrator twice interrupts before providing another concluding comment for the reader. First, let us look at the story without the interruptions and the conclusion. It begins with a description of Jesus purging the temple in Jerusalem and saying, "Take these things away; you shall not make my Father's house a house of trade" (2:13–16). After the first interruption (v. 17), the story continues with the "Jews" asking Jesus for a sign that would justify what he did (v. 18), and Jesus responds, "Destroy this temple, and in three days I will raise it up" (v. 19). The "Jews" then reply to the effect that he could not raise up in three days what it took "forty six years to build" (v. 20),[19] and with this the story proper ends, again without resolution apart from the narrator's final interruption and concluding comment. Without the narrator's additions, the story is about Jesus' failure to provide a 'sign' that was convincing to those who asked for one. They did not believe that he *could* perform the sign he gave them. This, however, is only the conclusion of the actors in the story. The reader knows more.

As we have seen, because the reader knows the prologue to John's book, the reader knows things that the "Jews" in the story do not know. While the "Jews" hear Jesus refer to the temple as his "Father's house," readers know that Jesus is "the only Son from the Father," and based on 1:10 they know that his activity in the temple is the true Light's coming to "his own home." Similarly, readers understand the "Jews" to be the Light's "own people," and their response as their 'not receiving' and 'not believing' him. So while the "Jews" in the story find Jesus to have failed, the reader understands that the "Jews" failed because they did not understand who Jesus was or the significance of his words and deeds. In addition, they take his words and the sign they refer to literally, and this is one of the points that the narrator makes.

Whereas the story itself focuses on Jesus and the "Jews," the narrator's focus is on informing the reader about Jesus' disciples, who are not even actors in the story, any more than they were actors in the story about the wedding at Cana. The first interruption in 2:17 follows Jesus' statement to some of the traders in the temple: "His disciples remembered that it was written, 'Zeal for thy house will consume me'," which is a quotation from Ps. 69:9 that resonates with the reference in the preceding episode to the future 'hour' that Jesus wanted to postpone (2:4). Appearing where it does, the quotation indicates that such acts as the purging of the temple would or did "consume" Jesus, and his death is explicitly referred to in the next interruption and in the conclusion. The narrator first says that the temple Jesus spoke about was the temple of his body (v. 21), and then, developing the notion of remembering mentioned in 2:17, he says that after Jesus had been raised from the dead, his disciples remembered what Jesus had said about 'raising' the temple, "and they believed the scripture and the word which Jesus had spoken" (v. 22). Two points call for our attention, one concerning Jesus' speech and the other the disciples' understanding and belief.

First, while Jesus' words in verse 19 have a literal, everyday meaning, and were so understood by the "Jews," the narrator's prologue lends a literal meaning to the notion of Jesus' "Father" in verse 16,[20] while in verse 19 the narrator interprets the word 'temple' as a metaphor for Jesus' body. As a result, the "Jews" are shown to have misunderstood Jesus because they construed 'temple' literally when it was intended metaphorically. They understood what Jesus was saying but not what he meant because they did not know what the word 'temple' referred to. Nevertheless, for the reader the metaphorical meaning of 'temple' is comprehensible because it refers to what John considers to be the empirical fact of Jesus' death and resurrection, and so also is the play with the literal and metaphorical meanings of 'Father' comprehensible. But only up to a point. For while Jesus here refers literally to 'his Father', in John's special language 'Father' and 'Son' are metaphors for the Other becoming flesh and, as we will see, 'resurrection' is employed as a synonym with other words that represent the reverse process of the incarnation, the return of the Other into itself. The narrator is therefore playing with language on multiple levels, and in so doing he raises new issues about 'understanding' and 'belief', for the disciples did not at the time of the event understand or believe any more than the "Jews" did, as 2:17 and 22 indicate.

Second, from the passages and issues that we have discussed thus far, it is not surprising that the disciples' understanding was less than adequate, for in John belief does not presuppose understanding. According to 10:38, belief makes understanding possible. What is surprising is that the disciples' understanding and belief were different after the resurrection from what they were before it. After the resurrection, they remembered what Jesus had said, recalled a scriptural passage that explained it, "and they believed the scripture and the word which Jesus had spoken" (v. 22). So before the resurrection they 'believed in' him, and afterwards they 'understood' things about him. Because this notion is as important for the narrator's message as it is for his system of characterization, let us look at some other passages where the same notion occurs.

In the story of Jesus' entry into Jerusalem in 12:12–16, the narrator first describes a crowd's heralding of Jesus as "the King of Israel," just as Nathanael had done earlier, and then he says that Jesus found a young ass and sat upon it.[21] To this he adds, "as it is written," and quotes a passage from Zech. 9:9 concerning the coming of Zion's King, "sitting on an ass's colt." Then he makes a comment like the one in 2:22: "His disciples [who are not actors in this story either] did not understand this at first [i.e., "then"]; but when Jesus was glorified, then they remembered that this had been written of him and had been done to him" (12:16). Note that here 'glorification' is synonymous with 'resurrection' in 2:22.[22] A related passage occurs in 20:1–10. There, a disciple is said to have entered the now empty tomb in which Jesus had been buried, "and he saw and believed; *for as yet they did not know the scriptures, that he must rise from the dead*" (20:22). Because belief here explicitly precedes a subsequent understanding of what was experienced and understood, and belief has no content, there is nothing *that* is believed because it is understood.[23] We need only briefly comment here on the circumstances in which a new scriptural understanding occurred. It appears to be related to a post-glorification time that the narrator refers to in connection with the coming of "another counselor" (the Paraclete), the "Holy Spirit,"[24] or "The Spirit of Truth," who taught the disciples all things, brought to their remembrance all that Jesus said to them, "witnessed" to Jesus, and further guided them into "all the truth" (cf. 7:39; 14:16–17, 25–29; 15:26; 16:4–15). Whether or not the discovery of scriptures is related to this time, the distinction between 'belief' and 'understanding', and the association of the latter with the discovery, have three consequences for our reading of John's narrative.

First, because the narrator so self-consciously states that scriptures were only mined for meaning-giving texts after

40

Jesus' resurrection/glorification, when the character Jesus refers to such texts, as in 1:51 and 2:16, none of the other characters *can* have understood what Jesus was talking about. Second, Jesus is characterized as already knowing the scriptures that his disciples only discovered later. He not only knew them, but he also acted upon them, making them give special language meaning to words and deeds that is otherwise not apparent in them. And third, because scriptural knowledge is post-incarnation knowledge, it belongs to the encyclopedic knowledge of the special language shared by the narrator and his people. Indeed, they only learned the special language after Jesus was gone and after other events, such as the coming of the "Counselor" and the discovery of the significance of the scriptures for understanding what had happened while Jesus was with them.

3:1–15, 31–36

Let us now take up one last story in the sequence we have been following. John 3 represents both a climax to what we have seen thus far and a bridge to our next chapter, on what Jesus spoke about. It is a climax because it relates Jesus' speech to the narrator's speech in the prologue, and it is a bridge because it introduces a new semantic system to go along with those we saw in the prologue—the descent and the ascent of the Son of Man. Within John 3, we will for now concentrate on 3:1–15 and 31–36.[25]

The episode opens with Nicodemus, a Pharisee, and "a ruler of the Jews," coming to Jesus and, addressing him as "Rabbi," telling him that Jews ("we") know that he is "a teacher come from God," because he could not be doing his signs unless God was with him (3:1–2). For the special language reader, who has read the prologue to the book, the idea that Jesus has come from God, and that God is with him, is ironically true. But Nicodemus does not know the prologue and is unaware of the irony. Rather, like Nathanael he is operating with the conventional understanding of signs that we discussed earlier.

The narrator then says that Jesus "answered him," but his response disconcertingly lacks any bearing on what Nicodemus had said: "Truly, truly, I say to you, unless one is born anew [*anothen*], he cannot see the kingdom of God" (v. 3). Nicodemus's incredulous reply further links him to the literal-minded

"Jews" of 2:20, for he asks Jesus how a man can be born when he is old, if he can enter a second time into his mother's womb and be born (v. 4). He clearly understands "born anew" to mean literally "born again." Once more, however, the reader who recalls 1:12–13 knows that for John being "born anew" is synonymous with being "born of God," which is not, like literal 'birth', a matter of being born of blood, of the will of the flesh, or of the will of man, "but of God," whatever that may mean. But the original readers probably also knew that the Greek word for "anew" also means "from above," and therefore there is here also a play on double or multiple meanings.[26] However, the ultimate linguistic issue is not merely a matter of play with multiple lexical meanings, but it is a matter of what Jesus is *referring to,* and that is what he proceeds to speak about in 3:5–6, where he contrasts being "born of the flesh" with being "born of the Spirit," which resonates with 1:12–13. But 3:5–6 is as referentially uninformative as 1:12–13. Indeed, both of these passages present a superficial play on uses of the word 'birth', but on a deeper, special language level they leave the privileged meaning without an identifiable referent. This is the same kind of thing that we found in the play with literal and metaphorical meanings of "Father" and "temple" in 2:13–22. But it is also the same kind of thing that is operative in John's use of irony, as in the implicit irony in 3:2, where *we* know that Jesus is "from God" in a different sense from what Nicodemus understood, but also that "from God" is ultimately lacking in referential determinacy. Multiple meanings, literal and metaphorical meanings, and ironies are all play with everyday language, but underlying such play is John's special language, whose most fundamental characteristic is its radical blurring of referents, which in turn differentiates it from, and opposes it to, everyday language. John plays with everyday language by toying with the possibilities *in* it, but the ultimate play is *between* the everyday and the special language. And in John 3 he is far from finished with his play.

After Jesus 'clarifies' his meaning about being "born anew," he tells Nicodemus not to marvel at that idea any more than he would wonder about where "the wind" (*to pneuma*) comes from or where it goes, hearing only the sound of its movement. And then the two kinds of play come to expression when Jesus concludes, "You do not know whence it [the wind] comes or whither it goes; *so it is with every one who is born of the Spirit [ek tou pneumatos]*" (vv. 7–8). Within everyday language, Jesus is playing once more with two different meanings of the Greek word *pneuma*, first giving it its denotation of 'wind' and then giving it its denotation of 'Spirit'. In the last clause of the sentence, however, the play is between everyday and special language. To paraphrase Jesus' statement, he is saying, "Just as no one knows where the wind comes from or goes, so also does no one know how one is born of the Spirit."[27] The play with everyday meanings is over, and Jesus erases the referents of "born anew" and "born of the Spirit," much as he did in 1:12–13 when he defined 'becoming children of God' in terms of what it was *not*. But the play goes on, and in such a way as to assure us that Jesus is operating with the special language employed by the narrator in his prologue.

The theme of misunderstanding continues as Nicodemus again incredulously asks, "How can this be?" (v. 9), whereupon Jesus responds, "Are you a teacher of Israel, and yet you do not understand this?" (v. 10). This response is interesting because it both presupposes that Nicodemus *could* understand him and at the same time condemns a "teacher of Israel" for not understanding. In the case of the former, given the lack of ultimate reference to Jesus' words, it appears that Nicodemus should have understood that no one knows how spiritual rebirth occurs. In the case of the latter, however, Jesus' implicit condemnation is related to the social antagonism between special language people and everyday language people which we observed in the prologue. This is confirmed in Jesus' next words: "Truly, truly, I say to you, we speak of what *we* know [*oidamen*] and bear witness to what *we* have seen [*heorakamen*]; but *you* do not receive [*ou lambanete*] our testimony" (v. 11), to which we must add an expression from the next verse, "you do not believe" (*ou pisteuete*). Jesus' 'knowledge', which is based on what he has 'seen', is an echo of 1:18, where it is implied that he has 'seen' God, and explicitly stated that only he has made God 'known'. And Nicodemus' 'not believing' and 'not receiving' clearly employs the verbs used in 1:9–12 in connection with the failure of the Light's "own people" to 'receive' or 'believe' him.

And neither must we forget that birth is the subject of both 1:12–13 and the story about Nicodemus. All of these points therefore link the Nicodemus episode to the prologue and render the episode as an illustration of what has been said in it. Or, and more correctly, the prologue is the interpretive key to this episode, as it is to the whole of John's narrative. But the story and the play continue yet further.

The conclusion to Jesus' response to Nicodemus in 3:12–15 begins simply enough in 3:12 with Jesus telling him that, because he does not believe the "earthly things" (*ta epigeia*) of which he has spoken (concerning the wind), he cannot believe the "heavenly things" (*ta epourania*) either (i.e., about being "born anew" or "of the Spirit"). We have seen another version of such a statement in 1:50–51 in the story about Nathanael, and here, as there, Jesus speaks about 'ascent' and 'descent' in connection with "the Son of Man" (3:13). There, "the Son of Man" was the ladder between heaven and earth, upon which angels 'ascended' and 'descended', and this is understood as something that Moses had written about Jesus. Here, Jesus says, "No one has ascended into heaven but he who descended from heaven, the Son of Man." And then he says, "And as Moses lifted up the serpent in the wilderness, so must the Son of Man be lifted up, that whoever believes in him may have eternal life" (vv. 14–15). For the moment, what is important in this statement about Moses is that Moses and Jesus are contrasted in such a way as to render Jesus superior to Moses. This is important because it sheds some light on the statement in 3:13, in which Jesus denies that anyone has ascended to heaven but the Son of Man who had descended from heaven. To understand what is going on here, we must return once more to the prologue where, after contrasting in a subordinating manner the Law that came through Moses with the "grace and truth" that came through Jesus (1:17), the narrator makes a comment that is formally and materially related to 3:13: "No one has ever seen God; the only Son, who *is* in the bosom of the Father, he has made him known" (1:18). Several parallels between this and 3:12–15 need to be observed.

Clearly, there is a relationship between "no one has ever seen God" and "no one has ascended to heaven." On the one hand, it is asserted that no one has done either of these, and this sounds like a rejection of the notion that someone has. The narrator never identifies who this might be, but some Jewish traditions maintained that Moses had done both, and this would make sense of John's denial that he had, for he persistently contrasts Moses with Jesus and subordinates Moses to Jesus.[28] On the other hand, and positively, the narrator says that Jesus has made "the Father" "known," which according to 3:11 and 32 is his "witness" to what he had "seen and heard" in heaven, and the narrator also says that Jesus 'comes from heaven/above' (3:31). The contrast is therefore not only between Moses and Jesus, but also between 'ascending' and 'descending', and 'descending' and 'ascending'. Humans go up to heaven and come down, but heavenly beings come down and go back up. Moses did not ascend, and therefore he did not see God, but Jesus saw God and descended to make him known. Moses is "of the earth," and "of the earth he speaks"; Jesus "comes from heaven" and "bears witness to what he has seen and heard" (3:31–32). So Nicodemus did not understand or believe the "earthly things" of which Jesus spoke, let alone the "heavenly things." But Jesus' response to him raises a further issue.

In 3:13 Jesus refers to the fact that he had not only descended from heaven, but that he had also ascended to heaven. This is clearly a reference to Jesus' return whence he was sent, and for this reason it reflects the narrator's post-'resurrection' point of view, the same point of view taken up by the narrator in 1:18, where he refers to the Son who had made the Father known as being back in the bosom of the Father.[29] More curious than this, however, is the suggestion in 3:15 that the Son of Man must be "lifted up" so that "whoever believes in him may have eternal life." Up to now, 'belief' has been a prerequisite for gaining 'eternal life', but here it is suggested that eternal life was not possible until after Jesus was 'lifted up'. To see what this is all about, we have to return to 3:14, where we must first examine the notion of being 'lifted up', because it could mean that eternal life is dependent on Jesus' crucifixion (12:32–33).

In 3:14 we have another play on multiple meanings *within* everyday language, but also, in the light of 3:13, 16–21, and 31–36, a play *between* everyday language and John's special language. Within everyday language, the Greek verb *hypsoo* is first used in the sense of 'lifting up' appropriate to Moses' 'holding up' the serpent, and then in the sense of Jesus himself being 'lifted up', denoting his crucifixion, as is clearly implied in 8:38, where "Jews" (8:22) are the ones who will 'lift up' the Son of Man, Jesus, and in 12:33 Jesus' being 'lifted up' is explicitly interpreted as a reference to the means by which Jesus died.[30] On the other hand, however, there is also a play between everyday language and special language, as we can see from 3:13, where there is an implied relationship between the Son of Man's 'ascent' and Jesus' being 'lifted up'. And there is a related play in the context of the statement of 8:38, which has to do with where 'Jesus' has come from and where he is going, matters that the "Jews" do not understand because they are thinking in everyday terms, judging Jesus "according to the flesh" (8:14–15). Consequently, when Jesus speaks about 'going away', they think he might be referring to his killing himself (8:21–22). But Jesus then makes the special language point: "You are from below. I am from above; you are of this world, I am not of this world" (8:23). Jesus' 'going away' is therefore not a reference to suicide, but to his return to the place 'above' whence he came. But by the same token, his being "lifted up" by the "Jews" refers in everyday language to the mode of his execution, but in John's special language it refers to the return of the Word from its incarnation. In the words of 12:23, it is "the hour . . . for the Son of Man to be *glorified*," which is expressed in everyday language in 12:32 when Jesus refers to his being "lifted up *from the earth*,"[31] and in the special language in 12:34 when Jesus is quoted as saying that "it is necessary for the Son of Man to be lifted up." The parallelism between 12:23 and 12:34 suggests that in the latter 'lifted up' has the denotation of 'exaltation'. What is more, in 6:52 Jesus refers to "the Son of Man ascending where he was before," thus rendering 'glorification' synonymous with both 'ascension' and 'exaltation'.

The special language synonymity among being 'lifted up', 'glorify', and 'ascend' points to the first verb's denotation of 'exaltation', 'making high', and guarantees that in 3:14b 'lifted up' is being used to refer to *both* the means of Jesus' death and his 'glorification'. However, because Jesus' death is included in the notion of being 'lifted up', it is also included in the special language meaning of 'glorify'. It belongs to the process of Jesus' 'glorification'. The denotation of 'exaltation' therefore includes both Jesus' crucifixion and his 'glorification'. But so also is Jesus' resurrection, for in 2:22 and 12:16 resurrection and glorification are synonymous.[32]

Thus, the fact remains that in John's special language there is no more of a possibility of understanding Jesus' coming and going than there is of understanding the wind's coming and going (3:8). 'Exaltation', 'glorification, 'resurrection', and 'ascent' all have different meanings, denotations, and referents in everyday language, but in John's special language they refer to the same thing, which is none of the things the words conventionally denote. And for this reason we cannot pin down their Johannine meaning and reference in anything but the minimal structural sense of the Word's return from its incarnation, namely the resumption of the state of glory that was obtained before the creation of the world (17:5, 24).

John 3:14 therefore means that eternal life becomes possible both after and because of Jesus' glorification. To understand this new prerequisite for eternal life, we must again remember the narrator's post-incarnation temporal point of view. From this point of view, he would appear to be saying that prior to Jesus' glorification believers had eternal life as a possibility that could only be realized after his glorification. On the other hand, because he is writing after the glorification and after Jesus' 'ascension', at a time when Jesus is back "in the bosom of the Father," the condition of glorification *has been met*. And therefore he can speak about believers in Jesus' time as *having* eternal life then (e.g., 3:36; 5:34; 6:47), just as he can retroject scriptural quotations and allusions back into the time of Jesus, even though the scriptures did not become known until after his glorification. Indeed, the narrator's retrospective point of view is doubtless also the reason for his representation of the disciples' less than adequate belief and understanding prior to Jesus' glorification. Before it, they did not 'believe' or 'understand' in the sense of 'belief' and 'understanding' that they enjoyed after it.[33]

Finally, we conclude our commentary on individual episodes with a passage in which the problem of language is explicitly addressed. The discourse in 3:31–36 appears as a continuation of the words of the Baptist in 3:25–30, just as the discourse in 3:16–21 appears to be a continuation of Jesus' words to Nicodemus. However, because both 3:16–21 and

3:31–36 are clearly in the special language of the narrator's discourse in 1:1–18, we should construe them as his direct address to his readers. In our discussion of the contrast between Jesus and Moses in 3:13–14, we have already mentioned the critical distinction made in 3:31–36, but now we must look at it again in light of the distinction between everyday and special language. Everyday language is referred to when the narrator says that "he who is of the earth belongs to the earth, and *of the earth he speaks*" (3:31b). He talks about "earthly things" (3:12). That is to say, human language denotes earthly things and it is used to refer to them. Indeed, it is *designed* to do so. But "he who comes from above . . . bears witness to what he has seen and heard . . . he . . . utters the words of God" (3:31–34). He speaks about "heavenly things" (3:12). So far, so good, but the narrator does not openly address the problem that he who comes from above and speaks of heavenly things does so in human language, which was not designed to denote and refer to heavenly things. And therefore his use of human language is necessarily different from everyday usage, as some characters in John's story observed when they reported that "no man ever spoke like this man!" (7:46).

In our discussion of the prologue and of the episodes in John 1:19–3:36, we have seen a variety of ways in which the narrator has developed a special use of everyday language in order to speak about 'heavenly things'. The key to this special use of language is provided in 3:31–34, and that key is its reference to heavenly rather than to earthly things. The different referents of the special language underlie all of the forms of play within the realm of everyday language, play with ambiguity, multiple meaning, irony, and literal and metaphorical reference. And because this play is dramatized in the encounter between various characters, the problem of reference is at issue in the repeated demonstrations of misunderstanding and of understandings, like those of the Baptist, disciples, and Nathanael, that are ironically correct for the reader who knows the special language, although they are wrong in the everyday understanding of the characters themselves.

We can now draw to a close our consideration of how Jesus speaks by entertaining the contrast between figurative and plain speech, which is the narrator's most explicit and self-conscious dramatization of Jesus' special use of language.

Figurative Speech versus Plain Speech

Several times, Jesus is said to have spoken 'figuratively' (*en paroimiais*) rather than 'plainly' or 'literally' (*en parresia;* 16:25, 29; 10:6; 11:14). But speaking *en parresia* again represents two different meanings. In one, it is contrasted with speaking "in secret" or "privately," and means 'openly' or 'publicly' (7:4, 13, 26; 18:20; cf. 10:54). In the other, it is contrasted with speaking 'figuratively' or in figures (*en paroimiais*), and means 'plainly', implying 'literally' (10:24; 11:14; 16:25, 29). When Jesus speaks 'figuratively', he is speaking in the special language. John 16 is especially interesting in this regard.

At the end of a discourse to his disciples about his 'return to the Father' (16:4b–15), Jesus says, "A little while, and you will see me no more; again a little while, and you will see me" (16:16; cf. 7:32–35; 8:21–22; 13:33, 36–37; 14:18–20, 28; 16:5). In reaction to the discourse, the disciples ask among themselves about what Jesus is saying to them; they "do not know what he is saying (*ouk oidamen ti lalei;* 16:17–18). More accurately, they do not know what he 'means' because they do not understand what he is referring to, any more than others did when they understood Jesus' 'going away' as a reference to his killing himself (8:21–22) or to his going off to "teach the Greeks" (7:32–35). Similarly, after Jesus speaks about his going to a place where his disciples cannot go, Peter asks "where" he is going and cannot understand why he cannot go there with him (13:33, 36–37), and in a related context Thomas tells Jesus that the disciples do not know where he is going, let alone how to get there (14:1–6). In all of these cases, characters other than Jesus do not know what he is referring to in his use of everyday language.

Jesus then responds to the disciples' questioning, and after a not very lucid explanation (16:19–24) he tells them that he has been speaking to them "in figures" (*en paroimiais*), but that soon he will speak to them "plainly" (*parresia*) about the Father (16:25). After a few more words, he concludes, "I came from the Father and have come into the world; again, I am leaving the world and going to the Father" (16:28). Upon hearing this, his disciples respond, "Ah, now you are speaking plainly [*en parresia*], not in any figure [*paroimian oudemian*]!" (16:29), and they proceed to profess that now they "understand" (*oidamen*) that he is omniscient and for this reason (*en touto*) 'believe that he has come from God' (16:30). In saying this, the disciples are speaking and thinking in everyday terms because they 'hear' X, 'think' or 'understand' Y, and 'believe' Z, which are the words Jesus uttered in verse 28. Moreover, what they 'understood' was that Jesus' omniscience was a Moses-like sign that proved that what Jesus said was true, and was therefore believable.[34] In this light, Jesus' retort, "Do you now believe?" (16:31), is unambiguously like his response to Nathanael, 'Because I said X, do you believe?' (1:50). And this is confirmed by the fact that in both cases Jesus concludes by telling his audience that they *will* experience something else, something that puts to question the claim of belief and the value of what was claimed to be believed (1:51; 16:32). But Jesus' figurative speech is not only construed like the conventional notion of sign; it is also understood to be figurative because it is found to be opaque when construed literally. In both figurative speech and speech wrongly construed in literal terms, the referent of the speech is either unknown or the wrong referent is assumed. This linguistic problem is evident in two other passages where figurative and plain speech are at issue.

In John 10, Jesus is speaking to Pharisees (9:40) and he employs an analogy about sheep, a shepherd, and robbers (10:1–5), following which the narrator tells the reader, "This figure [*paroimian*] Jesus used with them, but they did not understand [*ouk egnosan*] what he was saying to them [*tina en ha elalei autois;* 10:6]." Jesus then proceeds to explain that those who came before him were thieves and robbers and the sheep did not follow them, but that he is the "good shepherd" who will lay down his life for his sheep (10:8, 10–18). (For our present purposes, I will consider vv. 7b and 9 as interpolations because they obfuscate Jesus' explanation by making him the "door of the sheep" as well as the "shepherd.")[35] Jesus' explanation makes it clear that the failure to understand his analogy derived from his audience's ignorance of the referents of his metaphors of 'sheep', 'shepherd', and 'thieves' and 'robbers'. But his explanation also implies that the analogy could be understood if the referents of its terms were known. However, in verses 19–21 the narrator makes it clear that Jesus' audience did not understand either the analogy or the explanation.

A new episode appears in 10:22–30, but the narrator links it to 10:1–21 by picking up the theme of the sheep and the shepherd, and by having Jesus tell his audience (the "Jews") that they do not believe him because they do not belong to his sheep (10:26). Jesus draws this conclusion after "Jews" complained that he was keeping them in suspense and then said, picking up the narrator's comment on figurative speech in 10:6, "If you are the Christ, tell us plainly" (*parresia*; 10:24). Implicitly, the audience has been befuddled by what they construe as figurative speech and, like Jesus' disciples in John 16, they demand plain speech. Jesus says that he *has* told them, but that they do not believe, implying that he has told them in plain speech, although his final comments in verse 25–30 are all in the special language Jesus has used with them thus far.

A final example of the problem of figurative versus plain speech occurs in the story about Lazarus in John 11. In this story, there are two instances of Jesus' speech being a problem for his audience. In the first, he tells his disciples that the deceased Lazarus has "fallen asleep" and that he is going to "awaken" him (11:11). Like Nicodemus, the disciples construe his words literally and suggest that if Lazarus is only sleeping, there is no need to go to him because he will "recover," using a form of the Greek word *sozo*, which also means 'be saved' (11:12). At this point, the narrator intervenes to tell the reader that "Jesus had spoken of his [Lazarus's] death, but [that] they thought he meant [literally, "spoke about"] taking rest in sleep" (11:13), and then he says that Jesus told them "plainly" (*parresia*) that "Lazarus is dead" (11:14). Here, the figurative meaning of Jesus' original statement to his disciples derives from the everyday metaphorical use of 'sleep' and 'awaken' to refer to 'death' and 'coming back to life'. Lacking knowledge of the metaphors' reference, the disciples construed Jesus' words literally and misunderstood them, although their use of a verb for 'awakening' that also denotes 'salvation' may be a matter of the narrator's play with irony: they were right, but did not realize it. The possibility of such irony is reinforced when Jesus subsequently says that he is "the resurrection and the life," and that whoever believes in him shall live, even if they have died (11:25–26). When Lazarus comes back to life, he is implicitly 'saved' from death. There is a second instance of misunderstanding in this episode, but it lacks any explicit reference to figurative versus plain speech. Nevertheless, it further illustrates the problem of people understanding Jesus literally in the conventional terms of everyday speech, whereas Jesus' words are used in their special language sense. Now the reader and the disciples know that Jesus is going to wake Lazarus up, and that his 'sleep' is death. However, Lazarus's sister Martha knows only that her brother is dead and that if Jesus had been there he would not have died, but she also thinks that if he asks God, something could still be done for her brother (11:20–22). Consequently, when Jesus tells her that her brother will "rise again," she understands him to be referring to the everyday expectation (of some) that at the last day the dead would rise (11:24). Because she says that she already knows about this future resurrection, it is implied that Jesus' response was not of the immediate sort of relief she hoped for. She was looking for Jesus to raise him then and there, as he eventually does (11:40–44). But before Jesus does, the narrator plays with the problem of misunderstanding by having Jesus address the disappointed Martha and telling her that he *is* the resurrection and the life, and that 'whoever lives and believes in him shall never die' (11:25–26a). Then, in response to Jesus' question as to whether or not she believes what he said, she says, "Yes, Lord; I believe that you are the Christ, the Son of God, he who is coming into the world" (11:26b–27).

In addition to the play between the everyday and the special, the interaction between Jesus and Martha raises once more the question of the relationship between how people respond to Jesus and what their responses should have been. Martha's response is in this respect like the responses of the Baptist, the disciples, and Nathanael discussed earlier. It contains the correct words, but only if they are understood in their special language sense, and in this episode that sense is expressed in Jesus' claim *to be* not a miracle worker who can raise people from the dead, but "the resurrection and the life" in himself. Indeed, the notion of his being 'the life' is a link to the special language prologue, as is Jesus' comment that in Lazarus's coming back to life Martha 'saw' "the glory of God." In the words of the prologue, Martha 'beheld the glory of the Word' (11:40). Belief in everyday terms is acceptable because it is only in the everyday that this glory is manifest. Yet, the everyday is *not* the object of belief; it is only that in which the proper object, the 'glory', is to be apprehended and spoken about.[36]

We therefore conclude our exploration of how Jesus speaks and turn to what Jesus speaks about in speaking about the Other who is himself. And as we have had to entertain what he speaks about in order to comprehend how he speaks, so also will we have to consider how he speaks about the Other and himself.

Chapter 3

Language and Characterization 2: What Jesus Speaks About

He "who is of the earth belongs to the earth, and of the earth he speaks," but "he who comes from heaven . . . bears witness to what he has seen and heard"; he speaks of "heavenly things," not of "earthly things" (3:12, 31–32). "No man ever spoke like this man" (7:46), because this 'man', Jesus, is "not of this world," but "from above" (8:23), and he speaks differently because he uses a language designed to speak about earthly things to refer to heavenly things. And for these reasons, his language is as different from the everyday as his identity is different from the identity by which other characters in the story know him. As we turn, now, to what Jesus speaks about, and to its contribution to John's characterization of him, we are confronted by two related facts: Jesus' discourse is predominantly about himself, but what he says about himself does not match either what others know about him or what they understand of his speech and deeds. They 'beheld' a man they knew about, and they construed what he said and did in traditional terms familiar to them. Jesus, on the other hand, opposes his meaning to their understanding and elaborates his message by employing several different conceptual systems to make his point. Our principal concern will be with these systems, but we begin with the common knowledge and everyday understandings people have of him because his discourse is opposed to what they know and understand.

Common Knowledge and Everyday Understanding
To the characters in the story, Jesus is a Jew (4:9) from Nazareth in Galilee, and the son of Joseph (1:45; 6:42; 7:41, 52; 18:5). He

54

has a mother and brothers (2:1, 3, 5, 12; 6:42; 7:35; 19:25–26), and he admits to having been "born," presumably "of the flesh like others" (18:37; cf. 1:13 and 3:6). He was uneducated (7:15) and, at the time of which the narrator speaks, he was less than fifty years old (8:57; cf. 2:20, "forty six years"[1]). Because of his public activity, he attracted some disciples and became widely known, and his words and deeds led some people to identify him in terms of conventional categories such as 'teacher' or 'rabbi', 'prophet', and 'Messiah', while others, notably Jewish leaders, considered his words and deeds to be inconsistent with conventional expectations, so much so that they sought to kill him, and eventually they succeeded. So while some thought that he was a good man, others thought he was leading people astray (7:12, 47), and yet others considered him to be paranoid (7:20; 8:48; 10:19–21). But Jewish authorities saw him as a "sinner" for breaking sabbath laws (5:16; 7:21–23; 9:13–16), as a "blasphemer" because he called God his Father, "making himself equal to God" (5:17–18; 10:31–36; 19:7), and as a threat to peace, which made them afraid that if everyone believed him, the Romans would come and destroy both their holy place—the temple—and their nation (11:48). So they arrested him with the help of one of his disciples and turned him over to Roman authorities, who allowed them to execute him for having claimed to be "the Son of God, the King of the Jews" (18:1–19:42). His disciples, however, claimed that he came back to life and appeared to them before he "ascended to the Father" (John 20–21).

One of the distinctive features of John's characterization of Jesus is that Jesus never disputes the biographical knowledge others have of him, but rather asserts things of himself that appear to contradict that knowledge, such as that he is "from heaven" and is "not of this world," that he has been sent by his Father, who is not Joseph but God, and so on. John's Jesus has no problem in saying in one and the same breath, "I was born" and "I have come into the world" (18:37).[2] Be this as it may, other characters perceive him in terms of their common knowledge and of conventional understandings of what his behavior might signify. In our last chapter, we saw in connection with Jesus' Moses-like signs that many construed him as having come from or been sent by God because of the deeds he performed. And we found that, for the reader, these characters are ironically right in their interpretation—that Jesus has come from

God—but wrong in precisely what they understand that coming to refer to. Where Jesus comes from, as well as where he is going, provide the most frequent topics of stories concerning the misunderstanding of the common biographical knowledge. These are worth looking at, because they reflect the pervasive misunderstandings that are also ironically correct when their special language reference is understood. That is to say, the misunderstandings also point to what Jesus affirms about himself.

In addition to the identification of Jesus as a prophet like Moses, the problem of where Jesus comes from is also related to conventional understandings of from where the Messiah is to come. For some like Nathanael, Jesus' coming from Nazareth in Galilee means that he comes from the wrong place, because nothing good is expected to come out of Nazareth (cf. 1:46). For others, he comes from the wrong place because scripture says that the Christ is to come from David's village of Bethlehem, not from Galilee (7:40–42), and scripture says nothing about a prophet rising from Galilee either (7:52). For yet others, Jesus' known place of origin was a problem because it was believed that when the Christ comes, "no one will know where he comes from" (7:27). In a further play on Jesus' having come from God, "Jews" claim that they know "that God has spoken to Moses, but as for this man, we do not know where he comes from," that is, whether or not he comes from God in the same sense that Moses did (9:29–33; cf. 19:9, which may refer back to 18:37). And last, after Jesus has said, "'I have come down from heaven'," "Jews" say, "Is not this Jesus, the son of Joseph, whose father and mother we know?" (6:42). Jesus, of course, knows that his questioners do not know who he is, where he comes from (7:28–29), or where he is going because they judge "according to the flesh," "by appearances," not with "right judgment" (8:14–15; 7:24). That is to say, they judge him in everyday terms. So, too, the characters in the story no more understand Jesus' going than they do his coming (8:14). Some thought he was talking about going off to "teach the Greeks" (7:33–36), some that he was going to kill himself (8:21–22), and his disciples simply did not understand what he was talking about (13:33, 36–37; 14:1–6, 18–29; 16:5–31). None of the characters in the story have gone beyond everyday language and conventional understanding. But 'Jesus', the narrator, and presumably his people *have* 'gone beyond', and now it is our task to do so as well. We begin with another distinctive feature of John's characterization of Jesus, the incredible number of ways in which Jesus is identified by the narrator, by other actors in his story, and by Jesus himself.

Identifications of Jesus

In the two preceding chapters, we have seen a number of names and titles attributed to Jesus, and among them many that were synonymous with one another, either in everyday language or in the narrator's special language. And we have seen, too, that some names and titles that are wrongly understood in everyday terms are ironically correct when understood in the terms of the special language. For these reasons, a comprehensive list of all of the identifiers applied to Jesus will help us to see how we might go beyond the everyday and into John's special language. The following table contains all of the identifiers in a sequence based on the order of their appearance in the text, which is the order in which the characters use them and the reader learns of them. In order to see who calls Jesus what, each entry is broken down according to who employs the identifier: the narrator, other actors, and Jesus (see table).

Of these over two dozen identifiers, many need not concern us here. For example, some are everyday language synonyms or virtual synonyms that are of no special language relevance. Thus 'Rabbi/teacher' and 'lord' (meaning 'master') are synonymous when people use them to refer to Jesus as their superior or leader, or simply out of deference. Similarly, 'Messiah/Christ', 'king' (of Israel/the Jews), 'Son of God', 'Holy one of God', and 'Saviour of the world' are everyday language synonyms when used to refer to Jesus' royal role in the world, although 'Son of God' has a special language denotation when used by the narrator or Jesus. More interesting for our concerns are the possible special language synonyms represented in utterances in which Jesus predicates certain identifiers of himself by saying "I am X."[3]

Jesus says of himself that he is "the life" (11:25; 14:6), "the way" (14:6), "the truth" (14:6), "the light of the world" (8:12; cf. 9:5, 12:46), "the bread of life" and "living bread" (6:35, 48, 51), "the door of the sheep" (10:7, 9), "the good shepherd" (10:11, 14), "the resurrection" (11:25), "the true vine" (15:1), and "the

Title	Narrator	Others	Jesus
The Word	1:14; cf. 1:1–3		
God	1:1	10:33; 20:28	10:30, 38; 14:8–11(?)
The Life	1:4		11:25; 14:6
The Light	1:4–12; 3:19–21		8:12; 9:5; 12:35–36; 12:46
Only Son (*Monogenes*)	1:14, 18; 3:16, 18 (in the latter two instances with *huion*, 'son')		
Jesus Christ (with 'Christ' as a proper name)	1:17		17:3
Lamb of God		1:29, 36	
Son, Son of God, Son of the Father	frequently	frequently	frequently
Rabbi/Teacher		1:36, 49; 3:2; 4:31; 6:25; 1:8, 28; 20:16	4:26 (cf. 4:25); 10:24–25
Christ/Messiah	20:31	1:41; 4:29; 7:26, 31, 41; 9:22; 10:24; 11:27	
Jesus of Nazareth, Son of Joseph		1:45; cf. 6:42, 18:5a, 7b	18:5b, 8
King (of Israel/the Jews)		1:49; 6:15; 12:13; 18:33, 39; 19:3, 14–15, 19–21	18:33, 36(?) cf. 12:13–14
Son of man			1:51; 3:13–15; 5:27; 6:27, 53, 62; 8:28; 9:35–37; 12:34
Bridegroom		3:28–30	
Lord (as honorific 'sir' or 'master')		4:11, 15, 19; 6:68(?); 11:3, 12, 21, 27, 32, 34; 13:6, 9, 25, 36, 37; 20:15; 21:15(?), 17(?), 20–21(?)	13:13(?)

Title	Narrator	Others	Jesus
The Lord (as title)	21:12	20:2, 18, 20, 25, 28; 21:7	13:13(?)
a or the Prophet	4:44	4:19; 6:14; 7:40, 52	4:44(?)
The Savior of the World		4:42	
Bread of Life/Living Bread			6:(33) 35; (38) 48, 51
The Holy One of God		6:69	
a Samaritan		8:48	
The Door (of the sheep)			10:7, 9
The Good Shepherd			10:11, 14
The Resurrection (and the Life)			11:25
The Way			14:6
The Truth (and the Life)			14:6
The True Vine			15:1

Son of God" (10:36).[4] In addition to these, we should also add the one identifier that only he uses of himself, 'the Son of Man', although he never uses it in an 'I am X' form. Of these eleven identifiers, all but two, "the door" and "the true vine," are explicitly associated with Jesus as the source of 'life'. Four of them occur in two statements in which two or more identifications are made, and "the life" appears in both of them: "the way, the truth, and the life" (14:6), and "the resurrection and the life" (11:25). Moreover, the context of each statement insures that Jesus is the one through whom life comes (cf. 11:26, 14:19). Similarly, the "bread" is "the bread of life," the "good shepherd" came that his sheep "may have life" (10:10), and "the light" is "the light of life" (8:12; cf. 1:4). And "belief" in "the Son of Man" brings "eternal life" (e.g., 3:15), as does "belief" in "the Son of God" (e.g., 3:16–18, 36). In this light, we should further observe that "the true vine," which is not explicitly associated with "life," is a metaphor for the "Son" of "the Father" (15:10), and "the door" is a metaphor for Jesus as the means of 'salvation' (10:9), which means not only 'not perishing', but also *having* "eternal life" (3:16–17). All of the eleven self-predications therefore refer to Jesus as the one through whom 'life' comes. But does this mean that they are used synonymously in John's special language?

The eleven identifiers clearly belong to John's special language, but not all of them are synonyms. The "bread of life which has come down [descended] from heaven" is a metaphor for "the Son of Man" who came down, that is, descended from heaven (6:25–65), and the "door of the sheep" and the "good shepherd" are metaphors for "the Son of God/the Father" (10:14–18, 25–30; 15:1). On the other hand, although "the way," "the truth," "the life," and "the resurrection" are all predicated of "the Son of the Father" (14:6–7; 11:4, 27, 41), they are not metaphors that are saying that Jesus is like what these words denote in everyday language, as in Jesus being like "the bread of life" or like a "good shepherd." Rather, they are being used to say that Jesus *is* these things. That Jesus *is* "the resurrection" is different from saying that he is *like* "the resurrection." And that "the resurrection" does not refer metaphorically in this statement is evident from the explicit play with the expression's everyday denotation of a return to life "at the last day." Jesus denies that this is what he is referring to and says that he is referring to himself. He *is* "the Resurrection" in the same special language sense that he *is* "the Life," and these words are special language synonyms, for if Jesus is not 'life' in the sense of 'last day life', he is 'Life' in the moment of his speaking. Indeed, he is "the Life" spoken of in the narrator's prologue (1:4), and this is confirmed by his claim to be "the Light of Life" (8:12), which repeats the wording from the prologue. And in the prologue, "Word," "God," "Life," "Light," and "Truth" (1:14, 17) are all special language synonyms for the Other, but in 11:24 and 14:6, "Life," "Light," and "Truth" are applied to the Other who *is* Jesus. And because "the Way" is used in conjunction with these terms, it must also be reckoned as synonymous with them, and perhaps also with "the Door," because it shares with "the Way" connotations of 'access'. But there is another clue to the special language synonymity of all of these terms.

That the application of these identifiers to Jesus is a matter of special language is evident because they have the same effect of reference blurring that we saw in the prologue. The referent blurring entailed in the notion of 'Life' is best seen in 17:3, where Jesus defines the "eternal life" gained by believers as *knowing* "the only true God and Jesus Christ" whom he sent. "Eternal Life" *is* this 'knowledge' *and* vice versa, and therefore neither expression has the reference and meaning it has in everyday language. This definition is pertinent because 'knowing the Father' is also at issue in Jesus' assertion that he is "the Way, the Truth, and the Life" (14:6), which follows upon Thomas's claim of ignorance about Jesus' destination, and therefore about the 'way' to it (14:4–5). Thomas is clearly employing everyday understanding to the interpretation of Jesus' words, and Jesus' words are clearly used in a special language sense. This is evident in the verbal links to the prologue, but it is also evident in what Jesus says next: "If you had known me, you would have known my Father also; henceforth you know him and have seen him" (14:7). "He who has seen me has seen the Father . . . I am in the Father and the Father in me" (14:9–10). Jesus and the Father "are one" (10:30). So Jesus *is* "the Way, the Truth, and the Life" because he *is* the Father in a pre- and post-incarnational sense, a sense in which there is no 'Father' and there is no 'Son', but only the Other of whom these three terms are synonymous identifiers.

The same referential muddle in John's special language appears in connection with the notion of 'Truth'. The incarnate Word is "full of Grace and Truth," which came through Jesus Christ (1:14, 17; cf. 8:32, 40), who came to "bear witness to the Truth" (18:37), which is God's "word" (*logon*) and is "true" (17:17b), and *is* God, who "is true" (3:33; 7:28; 8:26).[5] Similarly, those who are "of the Truth" (18:37; cf. 3:21) are also said to be "of God" (8:47), "born of God" or "from above," in contrast with those who are "from below" and "of the world" (1:12–13; 3:3, 7; 8:23; 15:19; 17:14, 16), "born of blood, of the will of the flesh, of the will of man" (1:13; cf. 3:6). As in the prologue, "God" is synonymous with "the Truth."

Let us now return to our list and to some of the "I am" predications we have yet to consider, for they open up some new insights into John's special language. Of the eleven identifiers employed in the "I am" sayings, we have found eight that blur their referents because they are either synonymous with one another or they are metaphors for other identifiers that are themselves metaphors ("Son of God," "Son of Man"). This leaves three identifiers that are distinctive in John because they belong to extended conceptual systems: "the Light," "the Son of God/the Father," and "the Son of Man." But they are also distinctive because their systems are related to systems associated with three more identifiers from our extended list, the "prophet/ Messiah who is coming/has come into the world," "the bread of life that came down from heaven," and "the Word that became flesh." Usually, critics deal with these identifiers as separate christological titles or images. My concern is to show that each identifier belongs to a conceptual system, and that these systems overlap with one another in such a way as to produce referent blurring synonymy, underlying which is a minimal narrative structure.

Multiple Conceptual Systems

These six conceptual systems and their relations to one another can best be appreciated by arraying them on parallel lines, grouped into three sets of two systems because of certain relations between the members of each set. Thus, "the Word" incarnate manifested "glory as of the only Son of the Father" (1:14, 18), both "the Son of Man" and "the bread of life" *descended* from heaven (6:25–65; cf. 3:13), and both "the Light" and "the prophet/Messiah" *'came into the world'*.[6] In order to highlight the parallels within and between sets, the major elements are indicated by key words.

the Word / became flesh and dwelt among us / (Jesus is glorified)[7]
the Son of God / sent from the Father / goes or returns to him

the Son of Man / descended from heaven or above / ascends to heaven
the bread of life / comes down = descends from heaven/——

the Light / shines or comes into the world / (darkness)[8]
prophet or Messiah / is coming into the world / remains forever[9]

Before we look at the three main systems in detail, a few observations are in order. First, except for the metaphorical "bread," each system is independent of the others in the sense that each could be used by itself as a model for representing and interpreting Jesus. This is clearly the case in the everyday understanding of the "prophet" or "Messiah," which is applied to Jesus by other characters in the narrative without their knowing about the other systems. But it is also clear from the independent use of these systems outside of John's narrative. Paul uses only the Father/Son system from our list, and Mark relates a Father/Son system to a different version of the Son of Man system, one that lacks a descent and an ascent.[10] And in the Jewish Wisdom tradition, which all critics see as closely related to the Word system, the Wisdom system appears independently of the others in our list, except for a very different version of the Father/Son system.[11] We will reserve discussion of the Wisdom system for Chapter 5.

The first observation leads to the second, namely that John not only employs all six systems in his characterization of Jesus, but he also maps different ones of them onto one or more of the others, and he often opposes the special language systems to the prophet/Messiah system which he attributes to actors other than Jesus. For example, in 3:13–21, 8:12–59, and 12:20–36 we find the Son of Man, Father/Son, and Light systems, while in 6:25–65 we have the Son of Man, bread of life, and Father/Son systems but not the Light system, although in John 9 we have only the Son of Man and the Light systems. On the other hand, in John 5, 10, 11, and 14–17, there is only the Father/Son system, and in John 4 and 7 only the prophet/Messiah system (except for "the Father" in 4:21–23). By way of contrast, in John 18 Jesus himself employs none of these systems, although he refers to his "kingship" as not being "of this world" and claims that he has "come into the world, to bear witness to the Truth" (18:36–37), which is a transformation of the traditional system of the Messiah coming into the world into terms belonging to the special language system of Father and Son. The point is that the narrator employs different systems in different combinations, and in any given episode he excludes one or more of the systems. Nevertheless, and as we might expect from the prologue, the Father/Son system is the dominant one employed for the incarnate Word, and indeed it replaces the Word system after the prologue.[12] But we must not be misled by this dominance for, as we saw in our first chapter, the Father/Son system is a metaphor for the separation of the Other from Jesus during the time of the Other's incarnation. And in this light, it would appear that the Son of Man system is for John also a metaphor for the same period of incarnational separation within the Other. This, then, leaves only the Word and the Light systems as nonmetaphorical, and because the Word system is not explicitly employed after the prologue, we are left with the Light system as the only literal form of reference to the Other during the period of the incarnation—of the Word which *was* the Light. But more of this peculiarity later.

The third and last observation to be made concerns the *structure* of the six systems, a structure that reflects an underlying narrative unity of conception beneath the diversity of expression. As the parallels show, apart from the bread system each of the others at least implicitly contains three elements: the *initial identification* of Jesus as "Word," "Son," and so on; a *transition statement* such as "sent," or "descended"; and a *departure statement,* such as "going" or "returning to the Father," and "ascend," but also in the implied special language 'death' of Jesus and in the implied absence of "light" in the return of "darkness." The departure statement is obviously the least stable structural element, because there is none for the bread system and the Word and Light systems only imply a 'departure'. Nevertheless, it is clear that in the underlying conception of the structure, John thinks of a coming and a going of the Other who for a time became Jesus: there is a birth and a death, a sending and a returning, a descent and an ascent, and light, like that of the sun, comes and goes. And we have also seen that John employs the notions of 'ascent', 'exaltation', 'glorification', and 'resurrection' as synonyms for the departure of the Other.[13] It therefore appears that the seeming instability of the departure element is only a result of the semantic limitations of the everyday language used in connection with the 'Word becoming flesh', for which no 'departure' or 'return' is semantically sensible, or with 'the Light coming into the world', for which there is likewise no sensible terminology in everyday language. The sun 'sets', and darkness 'comes', but 'light' has only its opposite, 'darkness', or it is 'put out'. And the notion of heavenly 'bread', which is to be 'consumed', offers no possibility of its return to heaven. These limitations only lend emphasis to John's creation of synonyms to compensate for them. Indeed, it is probable that the special language notion of 'glorification', which includes the fact of Jesus' death, serves to complete the Word system, because the 'glory' beheld in Jesus is the 'glory' of the creative Word (1:14), and because this 'glory' existed "before the world was made," and to it 'Jesus' returns, that is, is 'glorified' (17:5, 24).[14]

We turn now to the three main systems in order to identify their distinctive features as *systems*, but also to determine their special language characteristics. Although John maps them onto one another, we will consider them separately because each one has its own conceptual integrity, and because we can best appreciate John's mappings by understanding what he has mapped onto what. We begin with the Father/Son system because it is the most comprehensive and the most nuanced of the three. We will then turn to the Son of Man system, and then to the Light system, where we will consider especially its distinctive status both as a continuation of the prologue's representation of the Other and as an explanation of the distinctive features of the narrator's special language.

The Father/Son System

In 1:14–18, the Father/Son system takes over from the Word system when the narrator says that believers beheld the preincarnate Word's glory, "glory as of the only Son from the Father," and that no one had ever seen God, but the only Son who "made him known"; "Grace and Truth came through Jesus Christ." Subsequently in the narrative, the Word's 'becoming flesh' is also displaced by the notion that the Son was 'sent' by the Father (3:17, 34; 5:23, 24, 36, 37; 6:29, 38, 39, 44, 57; 7:16, 18, 28, 29; 8:16, 26; 12:44, 45, 49; 13:16, 20; 14:24; 17:3, 17, 25) and is 'going' back to him (13:1, 3; 14:12, 28; 16:5, 10, 17, 28; cf. 20:17, ascent "to the Father"). Nevertheless, the link to the prologue is maintained when Jesus says to "Jews," "His voice you have never heard [cf. 9:29], his form [*eidos*] you have never seen" (5:37b). No one has seen the Father except the Son (6:46), and no one has known him except the Son (8:55; cf. 7:28–29; 10:15; 17:25). Although the Son never describes *what* he has seen, he claims to speak of what he knows and to bear witness to what he has seen and heard (3:11, 32; 8:28, 38; 15:15), and this is a gift from heaven (3:27; 6:44). He does nothing of his own volition, but only what he has seen the Father doing and what the Father tells him to say (5:19–23, 30, 36; 6:38; 8:18; 12:49; 14:6, 24, 31; 15:10; 17:8, 14). Indeed, his words are not his own, but his Father's (3:34; 7:16–17; 8:26, 28; 12:49; 14:10, 24; 15:15; 17:8, 14), and these words "are spirit and Life" (6:63), testimony to "the Truth" (7:18, 28–29; 8:26, 32, 40; 17:17; 18:37). Likewise, his works bear witness that the Father has sent him (5:36; cf. 4:34; 5:19–20; 9:3–4; 10:25, 32, 37–38; 14:10; 15:24; 17:3–4).

The Son is therefore the *only* form in which the Father is 'seeable' and 'knowable'; to 'see', and 'know', and 'believe' the Son is to 'see' and 'know' the Father, the Truth (8:19; 10:38; 12:44–45; 14:7–9, 23; 18:23–24; 16:3). The Father's "word" (*logon*) is Truth (17:17), and the Son is Truth (14:6). The Son and the Father are "one" (10:30, 38; 17:11, 21). The Father is "in" him, and he is "in" the Father; the Father "dwells" in him and works through him (14:6–11). No one comes to the Father except by the Son (14:6).

Life was in the Word (1:4), and the Son who is the incarnate Word *is* Life (11:25; 14:6), and he gives eternal life to those who believe in him (3:16–17, 36; 5:24, 26, 40; 6:40a, 44–47; 10:10, 27–28; 11:25–26; 17:2; 20:31). His "words of eternal life" (6:68) are not *about* life, however; they *are* "spirit and Life" (6:63). 'Life' is therefore used both in its everyday sense of 'not death' (5:24; 10:10, 28), and in its special language sense of 'Life' as one of the synonyms employed to refer to the Other. The special language sense of 'eternal life' is reflected in its definition as the *knowledge* of "the only true God, and Jesus whom" he sent (17:3), a 'knowledge' that is synonymous with 'belief' because it is 'given' to those who see the Father in the Son and 'believe'. Thus, too, the semantic differences among 'life', 'belief', and 'knowledge' collapse because each of the words now refers to the same thing. And so, too, the Son can say that the Father "commanded" him what to speak and that this commandment *is* itself "eternal life" (12:49–50), and 'keeping' Jesus' commandments will lead believers to "know that I am in the Father, and you in me, and I in you," just as the Father is "in" Jesus (14:10, 15–20). 'Keeping' is here synonymous with 'believing' and 'knowing', but so also is 'loving' (8:42), for those who 'keep' Jesus' commandments 'love' Jesus and "he who loves me will be loved by the Father, and I will love him" (14:21). But this synonymity extends even further.

In the prologue to John's narrative, we found a number of special language synonyms for apprehending the Other in Jesus: 'knowing', 'receiving', 'believing', and 'beholding'. In addition to the further synonyms we have just observed, there are yet others. In 3:36, 'obeying' is synonymous with 'believing', but it is also synonymous with 'keeping' the Son's word, because both lead to "eternal life" (cf. 8:51–52, 55). And in 17:6–8, 'keeping' is synonymous with 'knowing', 'receiving', and 'believing'. But 'keeping' the word is synonymous with the word's 'abiding' in one (5:38) and with having the word of God "in" one (5:42). Similarly, 'belief' is synonymous with "doing the work of God" (6:29), which in turn is "doing the will" of him who sent the Son (4:34). 'Following' the Son, like 'belief' and 'keeping', are associated with receiving "eternal life" (10:27–28), as is 'coming to' the Son (5:40), which is synonymous with 'belief' (6:35; cf. 6:37, 44–45b; 8:47). The list goes on: 'honoring'

(5:23); 'hearing' (5:24; 6:45b; 8:47); 'judging' (7:24; 8:15); 'living in' the Son (11:26); and 'serving' him (12:26). In everyday language, each of these words or expressions means and denotes different things or different nuances of things, but in John's special language their reference to *one* thing, the positive apprehension of the Other in Jesus, undercuts their everyday meanings and denotations. They do not denote what they usually denote because they are used to refer to something else, something other, the positive relationship with the Other.

The otherness of this relationship is further indicated by a reversal or inversion of the process signaled by each of the terms in their everyday language use. In that usage, the subject of the verb or verbal expression is an active agent. The believer 'believes', the knower 'knows', the receiver 'receives'. John uses these terms in this everyday way, but in addition to his blurring of their reference, he also inverts their normal sense, as in such utterances as the following: "No one can receive anything *except what is given him from heaven*" (3:27); "No one can come to me *unless the Father who sent me draws him*" (6:44); "The Son gives eternal life to all whom *the Father has given him*" (17:2; cf. 17:6; 6:37, 45b; 8:42). The same kind of condition for being an active agent is expressed in such assertions as that "being of God" is a prerequisite for "hearing the words of God" (8:47), that only those who are "of the Truth" can hear Jesus' voice (18:37), and that having God as one's Father is a condition for being able to 'love' the Son (8:42). And obviously related to these is the notion that those who belong to the Son's sheep have been given to him by the Father (10:14, 27–29). In all of these cases, the believer is a *patient* of 'the Father's' action before becoming an *agent* of her or his action. Here, then, is yet another feature of John's special use of language, for the seemingly active agents of verbal expressions are only conditionally active. And for this reason the everyday sense and denotation of the expressions is further undercut.

Finally, 'eternal life' is of further interest because, as 'knowledge' of the Father, it entails a unity of the believer with the Father and the Son that is identical with their own unity of 'knowing' and 'being'. Until the believer dies, or until the Son comes again (14:3), they are in the world, but not of it (17:11, 14, 16). A time will come when they will be with the Father like Jesus is (cf. 1:18, 3:4–8; 10:14–18; 12:32; 13:36; 14:1–3, 18–20;

17:24). Then they will be perfectly "in" Jesus, and he "in" them, as he is "in" the Father and the Father "in" him. All will be one, just as Jesus and the Father are one (10:30; 14:20; 17:20–33). Believers will enter the Kingdom and see both it (3:3, 5) and the glory that the Father gave the Son "before the foundation of the world" (17:24; cf. 17:5 and 12:41), a glory that the Son gave to them that they might be one like the Father and the Son (17:22). Indeed, this "glory" is synonymous with the "word" (*logon*) that the Father gave to the Son and that the Son gave to his own (17:14). In his speech, the Son gave his Father's word, and in his works believers beheld the Word's glory (1:14; 2:11; 5:44; 7:18; 17:6–8). His works testify that the Father has sent him, but also that the Father is in him and he in the Father (5:36; 10:31–38; 14:8–11). So the Son came from glory, manifested it in the world, returned to it in a death to the flesh that was also his glorification (cf. 7:39; 12:16, 23; 13:31–33; 17:1, 5), and he will display it to his own in its original form when he brings them to where he is (17:24). But let us not forget that all of this is said in the everyday language of worldly differentiation, and that in the place of the Other there is no differentiation. This is, therefore, a special use of everyday language. The unity of Father, Son, and believers is an everyday language representation of entities and relationships that do not exist in the place of the Other, a place in which there is only the unity of the undifferentiated Other 'itself'. The Father/Son system therefore masks an ultimate absence of difference in the Other, which is differentiated only from the 'world'. More important, because the Other is present in Jesus, nondifferentiation is also present in him, as we will see in the Light system.

While the comprehensive character of the Father/Son system would have made it adequate as a single framework for talking about Jesus, the Son of Man and Light systems are much less comprehensive and, had they been used independently of others, they would have produced much different stories about Jesus. But John did employ them all, and he did so in such a way as to exacerbate the problem of reference that we have seen in the Father/Son system. We turn to the Son of Man system.

The Son of Man System

Although John interweaves the Son of Man system[15] with other systems, we can abstract it from them because of three key notions that are explicitly associated with 'the Son of Man'. The two principal notions are the 'descent' of the Son of Man from heaven and his subsequent 'ascent' to where he had been previously (3:13–14; 6:62; cf. 1:51, 20:17, and 6:27–51, where Jesus is "the bread of God" that has descended from heaven). The third notion is that of 'judgment', for Jesus judges "*because* he is the Son of Man" (5:27); "for judgment" he "came into the world" (9:39; cf. 9:35; see also 3:13–21 which is, however, interwoven with other systems, as in 5:22, 8:15–29, and 12:31–36). Nevertheless, the narrator describes neither the act of judgment nor its nature in terms of the Son of Man system, but rather concentrates on the 'ascent' of 'the Son of Man'.

As we saw in Chapter 2, the ascent of the Son of Man is related on the one hand to the narrator's denial that anyone had ascended into heaven but the Son of Man who had descended from heaven, and on the other hand to Jesus' death (3:13–15). Moreover, we found that both of these are related to contrasts with Moses. The denial that anyone else had ascended to heaven is a denial that Moses had done so (cf.1:17–18), and the Son of Man's being "lifted up" is contrasted with Moses' 'lifting up' of a magical serpent. In addition, from parallel statements about Jesus' being "lifted up" (3:14; 12:34), 'raised' (2:22; 20:9), "glorified" (12:23), and "ascending" (3:13; 6:52; cf. 20:17), we found that being 'lifted up' refers in everyday terms to the manner of Jesus' death, while in John's special language it refers to his 'exaltation'. Jesus' death is a part of the process of the Son of Man's return whence he came, which is a metaphor for the reintegration of the Other. But the Moses connection is also made in relation to the descent of the Son of Man.

In John 6, the descent of the Son of Man is elaborated in terms of the bread of life system, and in such a way as to form a bridge between the Son of Man system and the Father/Son system, for the bread of life is a link to the latter system's notion of 'eternal life' (6:27–51, 62).[16] Like the Son of Man's 'descent', "the bread of God . . . descends [*katabainon*] from heaven, and gives life to the world" (6:33, my translation of the verb; cf. v. 50). However, "the bread of God" is a metaphor for the Son of Man, for Jesus claims *to be* "the bread of life" that has "descended from heaven" (6:35, 38, 41–42, 48, 50–51). 'Eating' this 'bread' is therefore also a metaphor for 'believing in' Jesus as the Son

(6:35, 40, 47–51).[17] The Moses connection enters the picture because Jesus' being the "*true* bread from heaven" (6:32) is contrasted with "the mannah in the wilderness," which "Jews" thought was provided as a sign by Moses. Jesus claims that "it was not Moses who gave . . . the bread from heaven," but his Father, and that this "bread" "gives life to the world," unlike the mannah which only Jews ate in the wilderness, and died (6:30–33, 48–51). So as in the case of the serpent that Moses "lifted up," which is contrasted with *Jesus* being "lifted up," Jesus himself is "the *true* bread from heaven," which is contrasted with the mannah. Moreover, the contrast with Moses that involved his 'ascent' (3:13–14) is expressed in 6:46 in terms related to the implicit contrast in 1:17–18: "Not that any one has seen the Father except him who is from God; he has seen the Father." Moses would have had to have 'ascended' into heaven in order to have 'seen' the Father, but John says that he did neither. Finally, there is another parallel with the Moses tradition, in that as with Moses, so with Jesus: the "Jews" 'murmuring' against both of them is evidence of their failure to believe either of them (6:41–43; Exodus 16; cf. vv 61–64, on the 'murmuring' of Jesus' disciples). However, this shift from Moses to the "Jews" leads to another point.

Because the notions of descent and ascent are both contrastively associated with Moses, we need to take a further look at the notion of judgment in order to see if it is also related to Moses. Indeed, it is, but in a peculiar way. After Jesus said that he had "authority to execute judgment" because he is the Son of Man (5:27), he claims that his judgment is 'just' because he seeks not his own will but the will of him who sent him (6:30).[18] But then he shifts his focus from his own judgment to testimony that he expects "Jews" to judge, putting his audience in the position of judging the evidence of the Baptist and of his own works (6:31–38). In this connection, he refers to Jews searching the scriptures because they think that in them they have eternal life, and then he asserts that the scriptures "bear witness" to him (6:39). Jesus concludes his case by saying, "Do not think that I shall accuse you to the Father; it is Moses who accuses you, on whom you set your hope. If you believed Moses, you would believe me, for he wrote of me. But if you do not believe his writings, how will you believe my words?" (6:45–47). Here,

Moses is not contrasted with Jesus but is claimed as a witness to him. By this means, Jesus turns the authority acknowledged by the "Jews" against them and, as in the 'murmuring' of 6:41, claims that they are rejecting him just as they rejected Moses. The same point is made in 7:14–24 and 8:12–59, although the 'Son of Man' is not referred to in either case. Nevertheless, in all cases the issue of judgment surrounding the Son of Man is related to Moses, and in all of the cases Jesus' role of judge is displaced by a focus on the basis for others' judgment of him. We will pursue this inversion more fully in the next chapter. For now it will suffice to conclude that the Son of Man system is distinctively associated with play on the relationship between Jesus and Moses and on the ways in which "Jews" treated them both.[19]

There is one other distinctive feature of the Son of Man system that needs to be noted. If we view this system independently of the others, as 'the Son of Man' *Jesus* would be a preexistent heavenly being, one who, like angels, descended from heaven and then ascended to "where he was before" (6:62). In this respect, the Son of Man system is structurally equivalent to the Father/Son system, for the 'sending' of the Son and his 'going' to the Father parallels the 'descent' and 'ascent' of 'the Son of Man'. However, because the narrator interweaves these systems with yet others, the Son of Man system is as metaphorical as the Father/son system is. Both are metaphors for the Word system, in which it is 'the Word', not Jesus, that is pre-existent to its own incarnation *in* Jesus. But as we found in our consideration of the prologue, the "Word" is synonymous with the "Light," and this requires that we turn now to the Light system, for it entails a nonmetaphorical extension of the concepts of the prologue into the rest of the narrative.

The Light System

The equivocal equivalence of the Word and the Light systems is established in the prologue, where both are identified as agents of creation (1:3, 10), both enter the world (1:4, 9–10, 14) and, implicitly, both are the objects of 'receiving', 'knowing', and 'believing', or of their contraries (1:5, 10–12). The "Word" and the "Light" are also synonymous with the "Life," which is said to have been "in" the Word and to be "the Light of men" (1:3–4).

Outside of the prologue, the Word system is absent, but the Light system is variously interwoven with the Father/Son and Son of Man systems (cf. 3:16–21; 8:12–19; see also 5:19–46, which lacks reference to the Light but echoes elements of the other two passages). Although it is difficult to separate the Light system from these, two aspects of it are identifiable, one having to do with nondifferentiation, the other with differentiation, both of which are present in the prologue. There, the words 'Word', 'God', 'Life', and 'Light' do not differentiate referents, while the Light's shining in the world produces the differentiation between those who 'receive' and those who do not 'receive' the Light. By the same token, while the Other is itself undifferentiated, it is the originator of "the world," which is both differentiated from the Other and in itself the place of differentiation. And it is for this reason that once the Other enters the world it is spoken of in the language of differentiation, such as that of the 'sending of the Son', of the 'descent of the Son of Man', and of the 'Light shining in the world'. However, unlike 'sending', 'descending', and 'ascending', which are terms derived from the text, 'differentiation' and 'nondifferentiation' are analytical categories that describe the principal functions of the Light system. The Light system *creates* both differentiation and nondifferentiation, while the other two metaphorical systems *represent* them in anthropomorphic terms. To be sure, the *terms* of the Light system necessarily derive from everyday language, but the referents of these terms are, or derive from, the Other. Indeed, its terms are the closest to a language of the Other that everyday language can provide. Let us see.

Outside the prologue, differentiation is evident when we read that Jesus claims to *be* the Light that has come into the world (3:19; 8:12; 9:5; 12:46; cf. 1:9–13) to give "the Light of Life" to those who 'follow' (8:12) or 'believe in' that Light, which enables them to "become sons of Light" (12:36; cf. 12:49–50). To *have* "the Light of Life" is synonymous not only with being "sons of Light," but also with being "children of God" (1:12–13) and being "born anew" (3:3, 7), and all of these are synonymous with *having* 'eternal life' (cf. 3:16–21; 12:44–50), which is itself synonymous with *knowing* "the only true God and Jesus Christ" whom he sent (17:3). In the world and in its everyday language, 'God', 'Jesus', and 'believers' are differentiated from one another, but in John's special language synonymity the nondifferentiation of pre- and post-incarnational times penetrates even the time of the incarnation. Thus, "the Father has Life in himself" and "he has granted the Son also to have Life in himself" (5:26), while the Son claims to *be* the Life (11:25; 14:6) and gives Life to believers (e.g., 3:36; 5:24). Life, which was in the pre-incarnate Word as "the Light of men" (1:4), is during the time of the incarnation an undifferentiated commonality between the temporarily differentiated Father, Son, and children of God, and it is present both *in* Jesus as the incarnate Word, and *in* those who believe in him and therefore already have eternal life. But the notion of Light has its own peculiar quality of ultimate nondifferentiation before, during, and after the time of the incarnation.

The Other *is* Light both prior to the incarnation and during it, although during it Light's luminosity is only perceivable to belief (cf. 1:8–9; 12:36, 46), and then in terms of the Word's glory which is manifest in Jesus (cf. 1:14; 2:11). In this context, "glory" refers to the luminosity of the Word/Light that pre-existed Jesus (1:14; 12:41), even from before "the world was made," and to which it returned in Jesus' 'glorification' (17:1, 5, 24). In the time of the incarnation, this glory was manifest to 'belief' in Jesus' 'signs' (1:14; 2:11), and as the Father gave him his 'glory', so did he give it to his followers, so that they may be undifferentiatedly united both with one another and with the Father and the Son, even as the Father and the Son are themselves united (17:11, 20–24). To be sure, under the conditions of life in the world Father, Son, and the Father's children *are* differentiated from one another, but the ultimate state envisioned by John is the undifferentiated one referred to in the notions of 'Light', 'glory', and 'Life' (17:24; cf. 12:31–32; 14:2–3, 19–20). And because the believer 'experiences' all of these in the person of Jesus (cf. 14:6–11), they are present during the time of the incarnation.[20] For this reason, too, nondifferentiation is the key to John's special use of everyday language, the language of differentiation. Underlying the differences between entities linguistically identified by the 'Father', the 'Son', and the Father's 'children' is their 'unity' or 'oneness'. But what, now, of the differentiating function of the Light system?

The differentiating function of Light is related to the worldly distinction between day and night, which serves as an analogy for the Light shining in the world in Jesus. The analogy is a moralizing one associated with 'working' and 'walking' during the light of day rather than stumbling around in the darkness of night (8:12; 9:4–5; 11:9–10; 12:35–36). In addition, the transition from day to night is also analogous to the fact that Jesus, 'the Light', will not be permanently present in the world (9:4–5; 12:35–36). More precisely, 'walking' and 'working' are moralistic metaphors for 'belief' and its special language synonyms, and 'day and night' and 'light and darkness' are metaphors for the times of Jesus' presence and subsequent absence (12:35–36, 44–46). On the other hand, however, to say that Jesus himself *is* the Light that shines/comes into the world is *not* metaphorical. He *is* the "Light of this world" who also gives the "Light of Life" to those who come to him (8:12; cf. 1:4; 9:5; 12:46). But it is the coming/shining of the Light that produces the differentiation between those who have the "Light of Life" and those who do not. Like the sun, the Light makes differences visible. This is expressed in judgmental terms in 3:17–21, although the terms are somewhat confused by being interwoven with the Son of Man (3:13–15) and the Father/Son (3:16–17) systems. Nevertheless, the Light came into the world and in so doing disclosed those who come to the Light and those who do not. Those who come do so in order that their deeds may be seen, while others prefer darkness, lest their deeds be exposed by the Light. These disclosures are themselves a judgment, a differentiating *krisis* (3:18) in which eternal life and condemnation to death are determined by the very appearance of the Light (cf. 3:36; 5:24; 12:46–50; and 5:22–47 for a representation of this in terms of the Son of Man system).[21] For John, Light is first differentiated from darkness, which is the world without Light (1:1–5, 9–13), and then Light's shining in the world differentiates those who are of the Light from those who are not. No other system in John's special language repertoire so fully represents the "heavenly things" to which he refers. But we have also seen that the Light system is distinctive because it provides insights into the special language itself. This notion needs to be explored further, because of all the conceptual systems employed by John it comes the closest to *explaining* his special language.

The Explanatory Power of the Light System

John's Light system is dependent on the everyday experience of the light and darkness that is associated with day and night. This is evident in the solar analogies he uses in connection with Jesus as the Light, where Jesus is not solar light, but Light as such, and where darkness is not that of the solar night, but of the world as such. In 9:4–5, Jesus speaks about working while it is day because when night comes "no one can work," and then he claims that as long as he is in the world, he is "the Light of the world." In 11:9–10, he refers to there being "twelve hours in the day" and says that "if any one walks in the day, he does not stumble because he sees the light of this world. But if any one walks in the night, he stumbles, because the light is not in him."[22] Similarly, in 12:35b, he says, "Walk while you have the light, lest the darkness overtake you; he who walks in the darkness does not know where he goes." As in 9:4–5, and as probably implied in 11:9–10, Jesus here uses the experience of light and darkness as a metaphor for his presence and absence (12:35a, 36). This everyday experience also informs the statement in 1:5a, that "the Light shines in the darkness," although there the solar reference is erased by the special language synonymity of 'the Light', 'the Word', 'God', and 'the Life' which was "the Light of men." And solar reference is further displaced by the anthropomorphizing assertions about the Light in 1:6–13, in which *Jesus* is the Light as it came into the world. Both the relationship to solar light and the displacement are fully expressed in 8:12 in words that resonate with those of the prologue: "I am the Light of the world; he who follows me will not walk in darkness, but will have the Light of Life."

The experience of light and darkness that informs John's Light system also provides explanations of the three principal characteristics of his use of language: the everyday language of differentiation; the nondifferentiation of his special use of this language; and the contrastive character of his use of both the everyday and the special language.

John's solar analogies indicate that light enables one to see where one is going and to walk without stumbling. By making things visible, it enables one to differentiate between them, maneuver around them, and work with them. In the darkness, one cannot work, one does not know where one is going, and one stumbles—because one cannot differentiate between things. So light's illumination of a space differentiates between the things in it, as we have seen in the judgmentally discriminating function of Light in 3:18–21, and this is the link between the Light system and everyday language, for that language names the things occupying the illuminated space, identifies their qualities and quantities, and describes their relations to one another. The differentiating function of light in the Light system is causally related to the everyday language of differentiation because language names the different entities and relations disclosed by light's illumination.

The nondifferentiating function of Light is not explicitly addressed by John. Nevertheless, because he appeals to the everyday experience of light and darkness, and because he talks about Light both as other than darkness and as it is experienced from within darkness, we must consider another aspect of the experience of solar light. For in addition to the sun's light shining down on things and differentiating them, even giving them life, we also can look directly into the sun, and when we do we behold in it no differentiation at all; and if we look into it long enough, we become blinded (cf. John 9). The experience of looking into the sun therefore corresponds to, and may well be causally related to, the nondifferentiating feature of John's referent blurring special language.[23]

There is yet another aspect of the experience of solar light that corresponds to the third principal feature of John's use of language, namely its contrastive character. Critics have long cited John's use of dualities,[24] but this is part of a much more widespread linguistic and conceptual characteristic of John's style. The experience of solar light accounts for some of the fundamental dualities in John's language and thought, but by extension it accounts for a number of others, so many others that it is better to speak of their *contrastive* character, of which dualism or dualities are but one instance. Most obviously, the experience of the sun introduces the contrasts between light and darkness, heaven and earth, and above and below. By extension, it is also easy to see how other of John's contrasts follow from these, such as the contrasts between life and death, good and evil, love and hate, and spirit and flesh. But some of these lead us farther into contrasts both within everyday language and between it and John's special language.

As we saw in Chapter 2, in John 3 the narrator has Jesus play with the multiple everyday meanings of certain Greek words. Thus, *anothen* denotes both 'anew', as in 'again', and 'from above' (3:3–7), and *pneuma* denotes both 'the wind' and 'the Spirit' (3:8). But in addition to this play on meanings *within* everyday language, there is also a play *between* the everyday meanings and the special language meaning, for the privileged meanings in both cases, that is, 'from above' and 'the Spirit', also function as terms in John's special language. The same kinds of play have also been seen in connection with the verb *hypsoo*, which denotes both 'lifting something up', as in Moses' 'lifting up' of a bronze serpent, and as in Jesus' being 'lifted up' on a cross, while also denoting 'exaltation', as in John's special language understanding of 'ascension' and 'glorification' (3:14). And in 3:13 we find both the implicit contrast between ascending/descending and descending/ascending and the contrastive negation of the idea that anyone had ascended but the one who descended. But the context of this wordplay also introduces the further contrasts between not only the heavenly things of the special language and the earthly things of everyday language, but also between believing and receiving and their opposites (3:11–12, 31–36). The whole of John 3 illustrates the pervasiveness of contrastive thinking and language, most of which have been discussed in our preceding chapters. It will suffice, therefore, to note again that like the contrast between figurative and plain speech, irony and metaphor also depend on double meanings or double levels of meaning, and all three types of usage play on the contrast between the everyday and the special language. And of course, one of the pivotal contrasts is that between Jesus of Nazareth, the son of Joseph, and the incarnate Word, the only Son from the Father.

On all three linguistic counts, the Light system has an explanatory power enjoyed by no other system in John's special language. The experience of solar light has given him much food for thought. But John and his people had other experiences and they thought about other things, too. It is to these that we must now direct our attention, for they explain what solar light and the Light system cannot explain, namely why John so devalued "the world" and "earthly things." There is no necessity for one to move from reflection on solar things to the value-laden contrasts John persistently and systematically makes, or to prefer the undifferentiated to the differentiated. To explain these preferences, it is necessary to examine the sociology of Light in his narrative, a sociology already introduced in the prologue's assertion that the Light's coming into the world enabled some to 'behold', 'believe', and 'receive' it, while others rejected it. We must consider the problem of the "sons of Light" (12:36) living in a relationship of opposition to "the disciples of Moses" (9:28), whose "father" is "the devil," "a liar and the father of lies" (8:44).

Chapter 4

The Sociology of Light

In one sense, the sociology of Light can be said to begin with the Light shining in the darkness of the world and producing groups of people who either "come to the Light" or "love" darkness and "hate the Light" (3:19–21). However, the terms of this statement belong to John's special language response to the social conflict between his people, who have "come to the Light," and those who hated it and rejected both the Light and those who came to it. The sociology of Light therefore has two aspects, one having to do with the *social situation* in which John's people find themselves, and the other with their conceptual *response* to it.[1] In this chapter, we will explore first the social situation as John represents it,[2] and then examine his response. Our focus in both cases will be on the ways in which John's special language response is informed by the social situation. We have seen that unlike everyday language, this special language is not comprehensible in terms of denotation and reference. We will now have the opportunity to see how it becomes comprehensible in terms of its contrastive difference from the everyday.

The Social Situation: The Sons of Light and the Disciples of Moses

The single most important factor in John's social context is that his people have been rejected by a society of which they had been a part.[3] This factor is important because it means not only that the social balance is weighted on the side of those who have rejected them, for they have the power to reject, but also, and conversely, that the rejected are a relatively powerless minority that has been forced to the fringes or interstices of the dominant society. Their response to their situation is therefore a defensive reaction to their social experience. It is a means of coping with that experience, and as such it is a means of resocializing themselves, for their previous social identity has been denied them.[4] Their response gives them a new identity, and this is already evident, for example, in the notion that the rejected disciples of the rejected Jesus are "the sons of Light," who *was* Jesus (12:36), while their opponents, who "loved the darkness rather than the Light" (3:19; my translation), are sons of "the devil," "a liar and the Father of lies" (8:44). The "sons of Light" have *seen* the Light, and their opponents are "blind" (9:39–41). But these identifications also reflect a further important factor in the social situation, namely the passion that exists on both sides of the social balance, a passion most explicitly expressed in the contrast between *loving* and *hating* the Light (3:19–20). And as the depiction of the opponents indicates, the passion of the rejecters' hatred is matched if not exceeded by the invective of the rejected. So we are dealing with a case of social conflict between the powerful and the powerless in which emotions run high, and John's special language response is informed by both the conflict and the emotions. And as we will see, this response is itself the only power of the powerless, for they have no political redress with their rejecters. Their response is not missionary fare, but the fare of communal survival.[5]

According to John, the conflict began with Jesus' encounter with "his own people," the "Jews," who rejected him, persecuted him, and finally executed him. John writes retrospectively about Jesus' experience in the past, but his Jesus also often speaks prospectively about believers, relating their experience in his future to his experience in their past. Jesus says that in his time "the world has hated" his followers because they are "not of the world," even as he is "not of the world" (17:14–15; cf. vv. 14–18), but at the same time he anticipates people in the future who will believe in him through his followers' word (17:20–21), and the book of John's "testimony" is written for these future people, who are among John's constituency (19:35; 20:29–31). Jesus' words to his followers in his own time therefore apply equally to those who become his followers after his departure. Indeed, John's representation of Jesus' experience with the world/the "Jews" is a paradigm for their experience with the same opposition.[6] And so Jesus can say to his contemporary followers that the world that hates them hated him first, and it hates them because they are "not of the world," for he chose them "out of the world" (15:18–19). God "loved the world" and sent his Son to save it (3:16–17), but the world did not "know" the Son or the Father and therefore it "hated" them both. In its hatred, the world persecuted him, and it will persecute his followers because of him (15:20–21; cf. vv. 22–25). Therefore, "in the world" they have "tribulation," but "in" *him* they can have peace, because he has "overcome the world" (16:32–33). His followers will be expelled from the synagogues and killed, but Jesus warns them of these things in advance so that when his predictions come to pass they will not "fall away" (16:1–4a).

In addition to Jesus' predictions about persecution, expulsion from synagogues, and death at the hands of the "Jews," John also tells some stories about such experiences in Jesus' time which, because the same conflicts are predicted for later times, are also lessons for the times of John's readers. Indeed, it is probable that these stories represent and address conflicts experienced by believers in John's time.[7]

The story about a blind man in John 9 is especially interesting because it brings together the Light system and the themes of reception/nonreception and of blindness and sight, and all in the context of the expulsion of believers from synagogues by "Jews." The story begins with Jesus' disciples asking him about who was responsible (i.e., guilty) for a certain man having been born blind. Their assumption is that someone, either the man or his parents, must have "sinned" for him to have been born blind. Jesus rejects their assumption and claims that the man's blindness was not the result of sin, but "that the works of God might be made manifest in him" (9:1–3; cf. 11:4, 40). Jesus then introduces the analogy of working "while it is day" and claims that as long as he is in the world, he is "the Light of the world" (9:4–5). It is as the Light that Jesus gives sight to the blind man.

This theme is picked up again at the close of the story in 9:39–41, and in terms reminiscent of 3:16–21. Jesus says to the formerly blind man, "For judgment I came into this world, that those who do not see may see, and that those who see may become blind" (9:39). Apparently in response to the last clause, Pharisees then ask Jesus if *they* are blind, and he responds by saying that if they were blind they would "have no guilt," but their claim to see reveals their guilt (*hamartia;* 9:40–41). Jesus' response is not very lucid, but when we remember the disciples' conventional assumption that blindness was caused by someone having sinned (*hemarten,* 9:2), the guilt produced by the Pharisees' claim to see suggests that they have become blind. In their encounter with Jesus the Light, the blind man sees, and those who claim to see have become blind (9:39). The blind man has seen and believed (9:35–38), but Pharisees see and do not believe; indeed, they consider *Jesus* to be "a sinner" (*hamartolos;* 9:16, 24) and the blind man to have been born "in sin" (*en hamartiais;* 9:34). However, we must remember that Jesus rejected the disciples' conventional understanding of a causal relationship between guilt and infirmity, and that it is the reaction of others to *him* that produces sight and blindness. For Jesus, sin does not cause blindness, but blindness, as demonstrated by the "Pharisees'" disbelief, renders them guilty—Jesus thus inverts the everyday understanding that guilt produces infirmity by making infirmity the source of guilt.

Between this opening and close to the story, John narrates episodes involving the healed blind man, his neighbors, his parents, and the "Pharisees" and "Jews" (9:8–34). In an apparent attempt to get an official determination of how the man received his sight, neighbors bring him to Pharisees who interrogate him concerning both the event and the man who healed him. At issue throughout is the question whether or not a sign had been performed which proved that Jesus was a prophet "from God" (9:16–17, 24–33). The authorities did not believe that the man had been blind, that Jesus had performed the act, or that he was a prophet who, like Moses, was "from God," not least of all because Jesus had acted on the sabbath, which led them to judge him "a sinner." Most significant here is the fact that the Pharisees are acting in a judicial capacity that leads not only to their judgment that Jesus is a sinner, but also to their expulsion of the formerly blind man from the synagogue (9:34; cf. v. 22). This means that the whole story represents a war of judgment, one in which the Jews find the blind man and Jesus guilty, but also one in which their judgment stands as their own condemnation before Jesus. Thus the everyday judgmental process is taken up into and transformed by the special language judgment created by their response to Jesus, the Light. The story therefore represents a special language *inversion* of the judgmental process in which the judges of everyday life become the judged. Related to this, moreover, is the special language inversion involved in the question whether or not Jesus is "from God," for they not only reject the notion that Jesus is a prophet like Moses, but they also fail to grasp that Jesus *is* "from God" in a totally different sense: he "came into this world" (9:39) as "the Light of the world" (9:5), and that is why the "disciples of Moses" do not know where Jesus "comes from" (9:28–29). But the role of judgment in this story is also important because of what it reveals about the social situation of John's people.

The story represents the "Jews" as making a distinction between themselves as "disciples of Moses" and believers as "disciples" of Jesus (9:27–28), and as having established a policy that "if any one should confess him [Jesus] to be Christ, he was to be put out of the synagogue" (9:22b). This official policy led the blind man's parents to fear "the Jews" (9:22a), and it led the Jews to expel the man from the synagogue for being a disciple of Jesus (9:28, 34), whereupon he professed his belief in Jesus and worshiped him (9:35–38). So Jesus' work precipitated a crisis that produced both believers and nonbelievers, and it resulted in the nonbelievers expelling the believers from synagogues. The nonbelievers, however, are responsible for the policy of hostile rejection of believers, and this is the social experience of the believers. The story in John 9 represents the special language response to this situation, a response in which the tables of judgment are inverted by exalting Jesus' judgment over that of the judges.

The same social experience, and more, is represented in 12:9–11, where "Jews" contrive to kill Lazarus, whom Jesus had raised from the dead and for which they also "took counsel to put him [Jesus] to death" (11:53). In both cases, the motive behind these plots is that "many of the Jews were going away and believing in Jesus" (12:11; cf. 11:45–53), which in 7:12 and 47 is expressed in terms of their "being led astray." This motive is reiterated in another reference to expulsion in 12:41–43 where, after a reference to Isaiah having seen Jesus' "glory" (*doxa*), the narrator says that "many even of the authorities believed in him, but on account of the Pharisees they did not confess it, lest they should be put out of the synagogue" (12:42, my translation; cf. 7:13, "for fear of the Jews"). Then, in a play on the meanings of the word *doxa*, 'praise' and 'glory', the narrator concludes, "for they loved the praise (*doxa*) of men more than the glory (*doxa*) of God" (12:43, my translation). The "glory of God" is the Light that has come into the world to lead believers out of darkness and enable them to become "sons of Light" (12:35–36a, 46). And as for those who do not believe in him, he will not judge them, but "the word" (*logos*) that he has spoken will be their judge (12:47–50). As in John 9, believing or not believing in the Light entails a judgment that for believers supersedes the judgment of the "Jews."

John 12:9–11 establishes a new note, however, because in addition to the policy of expulsion from synagogues for believing in Jesus, it introduces a policy of executing those who entice other Jews to "go away and believe in Jesus" (12:11; cf. 16:2 and 11:45–53). John therefore represents two hostile policies, one for those who believe and another for those who lead others to believe.[8] And it may well be that we should read characterizations of Peter's ambivalence in exactly this light, for on the one hand he vowed to lay down his life for Jesus by "following him" (13:37), and on the other hand he lied to his interrogators when they asked if he was a disciple of Jesus (18:25–27).[9] Be this as it may, from these stories it is evident that John's book, as well as Jesus' words, is designed to keep persecuted believers from "falling away" (16:1).

In addition to these stories, and because Jesus says that his followers would experience what he did, the stories of Jesus' own experience with the "Jews" must to some extent also mirror that of his followers. Like them, he is persecuted (5:16), and authorities interrogate him, seek to arrest him and to kill him (5:10–18; 7:1, 11–13, 32–36, 44–52; 8:12–20, 46, 48–59; 10:31–39; 11:8, 45–53, 57; 18:19–31; 19:7, 12, 16–21; cf. 1:14–28 on the interrogation of the Baptist). The systematic characterization of Jewish authorities as inquisitorial interrogators is doubtlessly familiar to John's readers, as is the response of "fear of the Jews." They are afraid to speak about Jesus (7:13; 9:22; 14:42;

19:38), to have their meetings known (20:19), and perhaps even to be seen in public (3:2; 11:7–8, 54). Even Pilate is afraid of the "Jews," and so accedes to their demands (19:8, 12–16). The climate of fear is further exacerbated by the fear of betrayal. Jesus is betrayed by a man whom he healed (5:15–18), and the blind man's neighbors turned him over to the Pharisees for interrogation (9:8–13). And, of course, one of Jesus' own disciples betrayed him to the authorities, leading to his trial and execution (13:21–30; 18:2–14, 19–24, 28–19:24). But the fear experienced by Jesus' followers is as much a fear of the hatred that motivates their persecutors as it is of expulsion and execution (7:7; 15:18–25; 17:14; cf. 3:20). Paradoxically, for believers to fall away out of fear for the loss of the lives they love will end up costing them their lives, whereas if they hate their lives in this world, they will keep their lives eternally. For John and his Jesus, the only solution to the social dilemma is to serve Jesus and follow him, so that they might be with him (cf. 10:12–15, 27–29; 12:25–26; 14:2–3, 18–19, 23–24; 15:1–27; 16:1–21, 32–33; 17:1–26). Nothing better represents the radicality of John's perception of the social situation, and nothing better explains why he preferred the heavenly to the earthly than the notion that one can only enjoy life eternally by *hating* life in this world (12:25). The social experience of John and his people engendered a fear that made life in this world hateful because it had become untenable. Having been hated by the world, they came to hate the world, which is yet another special language inversion.

This brief survey of the conflictual social situation represented in John's narrative reveals the basic characteristics of the situation, but it also discloses some fundamental features of his special language response to it. Therefore, before we pursue his response further let us reflect for a moment on what we have seen.

Two main points arise out of our survey. The first concerns the *polarization* of the social situation in terms of the disciples of Moses and the disciples of Jesus, and these poles are opposed to one another in terms of the political power of the former over the powerlessness of the latter. The disciples of Moses control both the political situation and the terms in which the politics are played out. What is more, these terms are the conventional ones of everyday life; they belong to everyday 'language', taking, now, the notion of 'language' in its broader sense of traditional social codes as well as in its narrower sense of the language as it is spoken.

Structurally, therefore, and from the perspective of the disciples of Moses, their language has a positive value and the language of the disciples of Jesus has a negative value. This leads to the second point, which concerns John's special language response. John accepts the polarization, in all probability because, as the rejected, he and his people had no choice in the matter, but he *inverts* the terms of the conflict.[10] He inverts the conventional notion of the causal relationship between guilt and infirmity, he inverts the understanding of the judicial process at issue in the social situation, and he inverts the everyday values of 'life' and 'death' and of 'love' and 'hate'. The result of these inversions of the terms of the conflict is also the inversion of the *values* the disciples of Moses placed on them. The poles are still opposed to one another, but John's special language, and therefore the disciples of Jesus, are valued positively and the opposition negatively. John's special language is a refraction of the social situation because the polarization of opposites and the inversion of terms and values derives from the social experience of his people. But as we saw in Chapter 3, they also found their principal reservoir of categories, oppositions, and values in the experience of the light of day and the darkness of night, an experience imaginatively elaborated in the absolute contrast between Light itself and the world as the place of darkness. The world's rejection of them has rendered it a place of darkness for them, and their only hope is in the Light that comes from outside the world.

The at least logical if not also historical process of refraction through polarization and inversion can be seen in more abstract terms that represent three states evident in John's narrative.[11] The first is the pre-incarnation state in which the world (i.e., the "Jews") envisions itself as the Same in contrast with the Other, which is "God." I use the expression 'the Same' to represent the facts that the people of the world are of the same kind and have the same traditions, language, and values, and that they conceive of 'God' as other than themselves. The significance of this expression will become apparent momentarily. In addition to this contrast or structural opposition between the Other and the

Same, the world values the Other as positive and the Same as negative, for the world is the creation of God and he rules it through the Law he gave to Moses. The second state is that of the time of the incarnation, but it also includes the social history of John's people. In this state, the world envisions itself as the Same, but now in opposition to the *others* who are Jesus and his followers. Here, the world has from its perspective a positive value and the opposed others a negative one. The third state entails a shift in perspective, indeed, an inversion of point of view, from that of the world to that of Jesus and his people. They are still *other* to the world that has judged them to be other than itself, but along with the shift in perspective the values of the opposed groups have been inverted: Jesus and his disciples are given a positive value and Moses and his disciples are assigned a negative one. Since this is a bit complicated, a diagram may help to clarify the process.

Contrast: OTHER   SAME
     1. God +   ← the world −
     2. Jesus and his followers − ← the world +
Inversion: 3. Jesus and his followers + → the world −

The pivotal state in this diagram is number 2, which involves the social experience of John's people and, in their view, of Jesus as well. To deal with the intolerable position of being rejected and persecuted, John's people accepted state 1, in which the "Jews" valorized themselves negatively (i.e., inferior) in relation to God, whom they valorize as a positive Other to themselves. But John's people also accepted out of necessity their own negative valorization as Other to the disciples of Moses in state 2. This point is critical, because the whole process of their response pivots on their resolving the dilemma of their experience. The resolution comes in state 3, where the valorizations of the Other and the Same are *inverted* from that of state 2 but are the same as in state 1: Otherness is now positive and Sameness negative. Jesus and John's people are, like God, positively Other in contrast with the now negatively valorized Same, which is the world/the "Jews." In state 3, the point of view from which valorizations have been assigned is inverted, but also with the ironic affirmation of the Same's own negative valorization of itself in state 1. The contrastive structure maintained by the Same in state 1 is affirmed but transcended by the inversion in state 3 of the values posited in state 2. In effect, and also ironically, this inversion also reassigns the categories of the Other and the Same, for now God, Jesus, and his followers are positively the Same and in radical opposition to the world that has become negatively other to it.

This process now enables us to take our inquiry into John's special language a step further, for everything we have seen thus far about his use of language and about his social situation renders his special language *the anti-language of an anti-society*.[12]

John's Special Language as Anti-Language

John's community is an *anti-society* because it understands itself as other to the dominant society that has made it other. The very identity of his people is dependent upon their being other, and this is evident in their special use of the everyday language of the society that has rejected them. But this language must now be seen to be an *anti-language* because it derives its terms from the 'language' of their persecutors. To be sure, John's community held certain beliefs in common with other Christian groups, but even these beliefs are transformed by the community's anti-language.

As we have seen repeatedly, John's special language terms are not meaningful by virtue of their reference, but only by virtue of their difference from particular terms of the everyday 'language' of the dominant society. Anti-languages are not different everyday *languages;* they are languages that differ from an everyday language as a special use of *that* language. For example, when Pilate asks Jesus if he is "the King of the Jews" (18:33), "King of the Jews" has a concrete reference in Pilate's everyday language. Jesus' response, however, is in anti-language because he accepts Pilate's notion of 'King of the Jews' but denies its everyday referent by implying another one that is *opposed* to it: "my kingship is not of this world" (18:36). Here the political referent is displaced by another one that is semantically constituted by its otherness—"*not of this world*." Jesus does not point to a new, concrete referent for his use of the word 'king', but rather points to its *difference* from the referent Pilate had in mind.[13]

We have observed a number of instances of such negations and reference blurring in our consideration of John's special language, but now it is time to narrow our focus and concentrate on the role of anti-language in John's system of characterization, for it *is* an anti-language system. Indeed, John's special language is totally oriented to the characterization of both individuals and groups.

The basic elements of John's system of characterization are represented in the social contrast between the disciples of Moses and the disciples of Jesus. Although this contrast initially appears only to be between two groups, it actually entails two other contrasts, one between Moses and Jesus and the other between the disciples of Moses and Jesus. These three sets of contrasts are interwoven throughout John's narrative, and they also appear to have a hierarchical order in which higher levels provide a basis for elaborating lower ones:

Moses and Jesus

the disciples of Moses and Jesus

the disciples of Moses and the disciples of Jesus

In our review of the social situation represented in John's narrative, we focused principally on the bottom level, although we also had occasion to relate it to the level above it and saw how John related the middle level to the bottom one by making Jesus' experience a paradigm for the experience of his disciples. Our concern now is with the top two levels, both independently of and in relation to one another. The narrative action takes place largely between Jesus and the disciples of Moses, who act on the basis of their understanding of Moses, but Jesus often speaks about Moses, both in relation to himself and in relation to Moses' disciples' understanding of him. Indeed, whenever Jesus speaks about Moses and himself, he takes his lead from what the disciples of Moses understand about Moses, and it is for this reason that what Jesus says is in anti-language: he opposes his reading of Moses to theirs. But perhaps a better way to state this is to say that what Jesus says is *anti-structural*,[14] because the understandings he opposes belong to the social structure and everyday language of the disciples of Moses. John's special language is an anti-language *because* it is anti-structural, as we saw in Jesus' response to Pilate, where 'king' refers to a social structural role. Our first task, therefore, is to establish the 'structure' of the image of Moses against which his disciples measure Jesus and against which Jesus speaks when he talks about Moses and himself. Once we have established the structure, we will explore the effect of anti-structural statements on John's characterization of Jesus, and then on his characterization of the disciples of Moses.[15]

The Image of Moses

The key notion in the image of Moses held by his disciples is that of the coming of a prophet like Moses, which is predicted in Deut. 18:15–22. On the one hand, this passage opens the door to other biblical passages that round out the image of Moses, while on the other hand it is related to another passage in Deut. 13:1–5 that is concerned with how to identify and deal with a false prophet. In 18:15–22, Moses tells his people that their God will raise up from among them a prophet like himself, and that they must heed him. He traces the history of his own prophetic role back to the people's request at "Horeb" that he mediate between them and God (cf. Exod. 20:18–21), because they were afraid that they would die if they again heard the voice of God and saw again the great fire attending his presence (cf. John 5:37–38). According to Moses, it was at this time that God told him that he would raise up for them a prophet like himself, and that he, God, would put his words in the prophet's mouth and the prophet would speak to the people all that God commanded him (cf. Exod. 4:10–16). God then threatened that "whoever will not give heed to my words that he shall speak in my name, I myself will require it of him" (18:19). Then God turns to the problem of distinguishing between a true prophet like Moses and a false one. The problem is introduced when God says that a prophet who "presumes to speak a word in my name which I have not commanded him to speak, or who speaks in the name of other gods, that same prophet shall die" (18:20). The solution God offers concerns whether or not the word spoken by the prophet comes to pass or comes true. If it does not, "the prophet has spoken it presumptuously, you need not be afraid of him" (18:21–22). He shall die (18:20).

Deuteronomy 13:1–5 (13:1–6 in the Greek version) takes the problem of false prophets a few steps further. Moses begins his instructions with the case of a prophet (or a "dreamer of dreams'') "who gives you a sign [*semeion*] or a wonder, and the sign or wonder . . . comes to pass," but who also says, "Let us go after other gods." Moses tells the people that they should not listen to the words of such a prophet, for God is testing their love for him, and that they should put the prophet to death, because "he has taught rebellion" against God, to make them leave the way which God commanded them to walk. Therefore, they must purge the evil from their midst. In view of the fact that Jesus is judged to be a false prophet, who claimed to be "equal to God," that is, an "other god" (5:18; 10:33; 19:7), and who leads Israelites "astray" (*planao*; John 7:12, 47), we should note that the Greek text of Deut. 13:6 reads in place of "he has taught rebellion . . . ," "he spoke to lead you astray [*planao*] from the Lord your God." We will return to the judgment of Jesus later.

From the passages in Deuteronomy, the first feature by which a prophet will be identifiable as being like Moses is that given in 18:18: God will put his words in the prophet's mouth, and he shall speak to the people all that God commands him. The prophet's speaking in God's name (18:19) therefore means that he is speaking God's words, not his own or in his own name (cf. John 5:30–47; 7:16–18; 17:7–8). He is a mediator, and this role is said to have been requested by the people immediately after God issued the Ten Commandments on Mount Horeb/Sinai. A number of features of the image of Moses cluster around this moment, but as we saw in Chapter 2, others also cluster around Moses' earlier call by God to be *his* agent, which is narrated in Exodus 3–4 (see another version in 6:1–13).

John's narrative represents knowledge of several points related to Moses' call:

1. When God appears to Moses in a burning bush, "Moses hid his face, for he was afraid to look at God" (Exod. 3:6b; cf. John 1:18; 6:46).

2. God tells Moses that he is 'sending' him to Pharaoh in order for Moses to deliver God's people (3:10; cf. the Father's 'sending' of the Son).

3. When Moses expresses reluctance about taking on this mission, God gives him a "sign" (*semeion*), which will be the coming to pass of an event that God predicts (3:11–12; Deut.

18:21–22; see Jesus' predictions in 13:19, 14:29, and probably 8:28).[16]

4. When Moses tells God that he will need to know his name if he is going to tell the people who sent him, God tells him his name (3:13–16; cf. John 17:6, 11–12).[17]

5. Moses tells God that the people will not believe him or listen to his voice when he tells them that God appeared to him, whereupon God provides him with three more signs (*semeia;* a serpentine rod, a leprous hand, and Nile water that turns to blood) that are intended to make the people believe what Moses said (4:1–9, 17; cf. John 4:48 and Jesus' sign *acts* as occasions for belief).

6. Moses then claims to lack eloquence, even to be "slow of speech and of tongue" (cf. John 7:46), whereupon God claims to be the one who makes people dumb, deaf, seeing, and blind (cf. John 9:1–3, 39) and then consents to allow Moses' brother Aaron to be his spokesperson: "And you shall speak to him and put the words in his mouth; and I will be with your mouth and with his mouth . . . and he shall be a mouth for you, and you shall be to him as God" (4:10–16; cf. Deut. 18:18 and John 3:34; 7:16–18; 8:26–27, 31, 47; 12:44–50; 14:24b; 15:10, 15; 17:8, 14, 19–20).

From these points, the principal characteristics of a prophet like Moses will be that he is one who is sent by God (and will therefore have come from him), who spoke to him and gave him his, God's name, the words he is to speak, and signs that will make people believe what he says. John uses all of these terms in his characterization of Jesus, and he thereby renders Jesus as a prophet like Moses. However, other characteristics are added to these in connection with events surrounding God's descent upon Mount Horeb/Sinai to deliver his laws.

According to Exodus 19, "Moses *went up* to God" on the mountain, and there God spoke to him, telling him, among other things, that he, God, is going to come to Moses, "that the people may hear when I speak with you, and may also believe you forever" (19:3, 9). Moses then "*went down* from the mountain" to prepare the people (19:14). After preparations have been made, God *descended* upon the mountain with thunder, lightning, and so on, and then Moses "*went up*" to the top of the mountain to hear God (19:20), who told him to "*go down*" and warn the people and *"come up"* again with Aaron, and so Moses *"went down"* (19:21–25). Two more points emerge here. First, God speaks to Moses and the people know this (cf. John 9:29). Second, and more important, Moses' 'going up' and 'coming down' the mountain is in the Greek the same language that in John is used of the Son of Man's ascending (*anabaino*) and descending (*katabaino*). Moses therefore ascends the mountain to hear God speak, and then he descends to report to the people what God said. However, while Moses goes up and down the mountain, God descends upon the mountain from an unspecified place above it, presumably from heaven (19:11, 18, 20; cf. "from heaven" in 20:22, and 19:18, where smoke ascends from the mountain). The biblical text therefore distinguishes between God's descent and implied ascent, and Moses' ascent and descent, which is the same distinction Jesus makes in John 3:13, 6:38, 42, 62. Like God, Jesus descends from heaven and ascends to heaven, while Jesus denies that *anyone* has ever ascended into heaven (3:13). Moses only went up and down the mountain.[18]

After God descends, he issues ten commandments, following which the terrified people ask Moses to mediate between them and God: "You speak to us, and we will hear; but let not God speak to us, lest we die" (Exod. 20:19; cf. Deut. 18:16). This is the basis for Jesus telling "Jews" in his time: "His [God's] voice *you* have never heard, his form *you* have never seen" (John 5:37b; cf. 5:38 and Deut. 18:19). On the other hand, while *Moses* heard God's voice, the biblical text is ambiguous about whether or not he saw God (cf. John 1:18; 6:46). Exodus 3:6b says that "Moses hid his face, for he was afraid to look at God," but after several chapters of laws following Moses' assumption of his mediatorial role, he is back to going up and down the mountain with various other characters (24:1–2, 9–18). The text is often self-contradictory, but two new points are made. First, Moses and seventy-three leaders of Israel are said to have gone up and to have seen and beheld God (24:9–11). Shortly, this claim will be denied. Second, we are also told that when Moses went up (ascended) the mountain, the glory (*doxa*) of God descended (*katabaino*) on the mountain, which was covered by a cloud, and that Moses entered the cloud and remained there for "forty days and forty nights" (24:15–18), while God gave him further commandments (25:1–31:1–18), the last of which concerns the keeping of the sabbath, the failure to do so requiring the death of the transgressor (31:12–15). The second point therefore introduces the notion of the glory of God which is central to John's understanding of Jesus (e.g., John 1:14), but it also introduces the idea that failure to observe the sabbath entails the death penalty. In John, Jesus' failure to observe the sabbath is said to be the reason why the "Jews" persecuted him (5:16; cf. 7:19–23), but it is also the basis for their failure to accept him as a prophet like Moses: "This man is not from God, for he does not keep the sabbath" (9:16a, 24–33). This conclusion is also a judgment that Jesus is a false prophet when judged according to the image of a prophet like Moses.

The narrative of the book of Exodus continues with a story about Israelites breaking the second of the Ten Commandments (Exod. 20:4) by making golden calves while Moses was delayed in coming down from the mountain with the tables of the Law (Exodus 32). Most of the story concerns the punishment of the people, but twice Moses intercedes with God on their behalf (32:11–14, 30–35), thus rendering him an *intercessor* as well as a mediator. In John, Jesus inverts this role and makes Moses into the people's *accuser* (5:45).[19]

In the next episode in Exodus we return to issues concerning the glory of God and Moses' seeing God. In Exod. 33:7–11, we are told that Moses set up a "tent of meeting," and that whenever he entered the tent God appeared in a pillar of cloud, which 'descended' and stood at the door of the tent while God spoke with Moses: "The Lord used to speak to Moses face to face, as a man speaks to his friend" (33:9, 11). The question of what Moses saw is picked up shortly after this when Moses asks God to show him his glory (*doxa*; 33:18). God responds by saying, "You cannot see my face; for man shall not see me and live" (33:20), but then he allows Moses a concession by allowing him to see the back side of his glory, but not his face (33:21–23; contrast this with Num. 12:8, where the Greek has Moses beholding the "glory" of God). So Moses does *not* see God's glory or face, and this is affirmed in universal terms in John 1:18 and 6:46: "*No one* has ever seen God," except the Son. However, the notions of 'face' and 'glory' have another role, for when Moses descends from the mountain with the two tablets, the "skin of his face shone [*dedoxastai*] because he had been talking with God" (34:29; cf vv. 30, 35). Seeing this, the people "were afraid to come near him" (34:30), and so Moses had to wear a veil to protect them (34:33–35). Apropos of John, therefore, although God talked to Moses, Moses did not see God's glory, and neither did the people, who only saw the effect of God's glory on Moses' face. Believers in Jesus beheld in him the glory of the Word, which "was God" (1:14; 2:11).

Of other features of Moses' image that are relevant for John, two must be mentioned here because they figure prominently in John's anti-structural responses, namely the association of Moses with the mannah in the wilderness (Exodus 16),[20] which in John 6 is treated by "Jews" as a sign that rendered Moses believable, and with the bronze serpent lifted up by Moses to give life to those who had been bitten by real serpents (Num. 21:4–9), which in John is related to the eternal life associated with *Jesus'* being lifted up (3:14–15).[21]

Having seen the essential features of the image of Moses represented in John's narrative, we can now turn to John's response to this 'structure' in order to see how it is generated as an *anti-structural* response to the "Jews'" use of the image as a basis for understanding and judging Jesus. We begin with the fact that although both Jesus and other characters in the narrative refer to this image, the other characters *introduce* it, while Jesus and the narrator react to it by qualifying it.

John's Anti-Structural Response

From what we have observed about the image of Moses, a number of passages can be seen to represent the introduction of the image by characters other than Jesus. Already in the narrative's opening episode, the notion of a prophet like Moses is introduced in the question agents of the "Pharisees" pose to John the Baptist about whether he is "the Christ, . . . Elijah, [or] . . . *the prophet*" (1:19–24). Then Philip, a Jew, tells Nathanael, "a true Israelite," that he and his friends have "found him of whom Moses in the Law and also the prophets wrote," and Nathanael's response, "Can anything good *come* out of Nazareth?," suggests that he knew what Philip was talking about (1:45–46;

cf. 7:52). The sign requested by "Jews" in 2:18 is, like Moses' signs, understood by them to be a legitimation of what Jesus had done, for signs are designed to produce belief in the doer of them (2:23). And so the Pharisee Nicodemus claims to know that Jesus is "a teacher come from God," because "no one can do these signs that you do, unless God is with him" (3:1–2). Similarly, the Samaritan woman knows the Jewish expectation of a prophet/Messiah[22] who, when he comes, "will show us all things" (4:19, 25; cf. vv. 39–42). And Jesus himself acknowledges the tradition before the official from Capernaum when he says, "Unless you see signs and wonders you will not believe" (4:48). Thus, some people conclude from Jesus' sign of feeding a multitude that he is "the prophet who is to come into the world!" (6:14; cf. "king" in 6:15). And shortly later "Jews" ask for a sign that they may see, and believe him when he says that he has been sent, and this occurs in connection with Moses' signs (6:29–34). On the other hand, those who do not believe him judge him to be leading people astray (7:12), that is, that he is a false prophet like the ones mentioned in Deut. 13:1–5 (cf. John 7:47). For them, too, scripture does not say that a prophet will arise from Galilee (7:52; cf. vv. 40–42, of "the Christ"), and for them Jesus breaks the Law by "bearing witness" to himself (8:13–18) and by violating the sabbath, which proves that he is not from God (9:16). Indeed, because he makes himself "equal to God" by calling God his Father, he breaks the law of Deut. 13:1–5 and deserves to be executed (5:18; 10:33; 19:7). Others, however, believe that his acts demonstrate that he is "a prophet" (9:17, 33), while Jewish authorities see this as further evidence that Jesus is leading people astray (12:10–11). So characters other than Jesus understand and judge Jesus in terms of the image of a prophet like Moses.

As indicated by the cross-references to John in our sketch of the image of Moses, responses to it appear throughout John's narrative. However, two related features of that image provide a focal point for anti-structural responses, the ascent and descent of Moses, and his seeing God upon his ascent.[23] The anti-structural character of the responses to these features is evident in three statements that first deny what the image attributes to Moses and then make positive affirmations about Jesus:

"No one has ever seen God; the only Son,[24] who is in the

bosom of the Father, he [literally, "that one"] has made him known" (1:18).

"Not that anyone has seen the Father, except him who is from God; he has seen the Father (6:46).

"No one has ascended into heaven but he who descended from heaven, the Son of Man" (3:13).[25]

These statements are anti-structural not simply because of their negative formulations, but also and, more important, because what is positively affirmed about Jesus derives its *terms* from what is negated. The assertion that the 'Son of Man' descended from heaven and then ascended on the one hand takes its terms from what was said about Moses' ascent and descent, and on the other hand it inverts the direction of the movement to a descent and an ascent. This inversion is the single most critical point in John's characterization of Jesus, because it distinguishes Jesus from the image of Moses upon which it depends: Jesus comes from heaven. This alters all of the other elements of that image, and not least of all the implications of Jesus having seen God. The assertion that the Son saw God also derives its key term from what others said about Moses, but for John Jesus saw God *in heaven,* and it is from heaven that the Father sent him. In both cases, the *terms* of what is affirmed about Jesus derive from the image of Moses, not from any speculation about Jesus that was made independently of that image. To be sure, other *notions* inform what is affirmed, such as that Jesus is from heaven and that he is the incarnation of the Word, but the critical *terms* come from the image of Moses. We will entertain some of these other notions in Chapter 5. Now we must explore further John's anti-structural responses to the image. Let us return to the prologue.

Although 1:18 does not explicitly refer to Moses, 1:17 does, and it does so in connection with Moses as the bringer of the Law: "For the Law was given through Moses; Grace and Truth came through Jesus Christ." The two verses are related because the traditions of Moses seeing God are associated with events surrounding his reception of the Law. John does not deny that the Law came through Moses, but he does deny that Moses saw God. However, the assertions made about Jesus in the two statements are also related in such a way as to qualify the traditional value of the Law. For the "Grace and Truth" that "came through Jesus Christ" is what the Son has "made known" about the Father, whom he alone saw. Because of the denial and affirmation of who saw what, the juxtaposition of statements about what came from whom in 1:17 is an anti-structural *contrast*. What Jesus saw is contrasted with the Law given through Moses in such a way as to require that the Law be evaluated from the perspective of what came through Jesus, rather than have what came through Jesus be evaluated from the perspective of the Law, which is the way the disciples of Moses construed Jesus. This inversion is typical of John's anti-language, and it, too, is a consequence of the idea that Jesus came from heaven, as we will see later in connection with Jesus and the Law. There is in the prologue another trace of the image of Moses that calls for attention.

Because the image of Moses includes the notions of the glory of God and the glorification of Moses' face, we must also see 1:14 as an anti-structural response to these motifs: "And the Word became flesh and dwelt among us, full of Grace and Truth; we have beheld his glory, glory as of the only Son from the Father." In the biblical image of Moses, the glory of God is the luminous form of his presence that descended upon the mountain. It is not only distinct from Moses, but it is also the luminosity that illuminated Moses' face. In John, the glory is that of the Word which *was* God and it came into the world in the form of Jesus, where it was directly beheld (by believers) in Jesus himself (cf. 2:11). And the Word that had become incarnate returns to this glory in his or its glorification (17:5, 24). Thus the distinction between God's glory and Moses is collapsed in the relationship between God's glory and Jesus, who takes up the role of the glory that descended on Mount Horeb/Sinai. Moreover, in the metaphor of Jesus being the "only Son from the Father" we have a representation of a unity that exceeds that between "friends," which in Exod. 33:11a describes the relationship between Moses and God (cf. 33:12–17, where Moses "found favor" in God's sight and was known to God "by name"). Jesus' sonship is therefore an anti-structural contrast with Moses' friendship (on which see Chapter 5).

Further anti-structural statements occur in connection with the comment on ascent and descent in 3:13. Two of them also involve the implicit negation of an implied assertion, and both are accompanied by positive, special language affirmations:

"Unless one is born anew / from above, *he cannot see the kingdom of God*" (3:3).

"Unless one is born of water and the Spirit, *he cannot enter the kingdom of God*" (3:5).

The two negative clauses are related to the notions of 'ascent' (3:13) and 'seeing' God (3:32; cf. v. 34, 'sent') because they reject the premise that one can "enter" and "see the kingdom of God" without a prior rebirth. It is most probable that entering the kingdom is synonymous with ascending into heaven (3:13), whether by Moses or by others doing so in imitation of him.[26] Be this as it may, the affirmations made in the two statements are related to the affirmation in 3:13, that only he who "descended *from heaven*" has "ascended," because for John one cannot enter and see the kingdom unless one is "born *from above*." The meaning of this phrase appears to be expressed in words attributed to the Baptist in 3:27: "No one can receive anything except what is given him *from heaven*." The notions of receiving and being born appear in the prologue, where those who are "born of God" are those who "received" the Light that came into the world and "believed in his name" (1:9–13).[27] It is the one who "descended from heaven" who made it possible for others to be "born from above." Therefore, the anti-structural inversion of the notion of Moses' ascent and descent applies to believers as well as to Jesus: "*No one* has ascended into heaven but he who descended from heaven," and he made possible *not* an ascent but a birth "from above." "No one comes to the Father" but by the Son (14:6b).

Just as the denial that anyone has seen God in 1:18 lacked explicit reference to Moses, but was linked to a statement about Moses in 1:17, so also with the denial in 3:13 that anyone has ascended into heaven. John 3:14–15 posits yet another contrast between Moses and Jesus: "And just as Moses lifted up the serpent in the wilderness, so must the Son of Man be lifted up/exalted, that whoever believes in him may have eternal life." The two statements are related because Jesus' being lifted up is in John's special language also a reference to his exaltation, which is synonymous with his ascent and glorification.[28] On the other hand, 3:14–15 contains two anti-structural contrasts, and in both cases what is affirmed about Jesus derives its terms from the image of Moses. The obvious contrast is between Moses' lifting up and Jesus' being lifted up, where what is affirmed of Jesus is anti-structurally derived from what is said about Moses.[29] Less obvious is the anti-structural derivation of the expression 'eternal life', which derives from the notion of 'life' in Num. 21:9. There, Moses' lifting up of the bronze serpent is a life-giving antidote for those whose lives were threatened by snakebite. This 'life,' however, is only a temporary affair and it has nothing to do with the victims' *never* dying, whereas Jesus' being lifted up brings *"eternal life"* to those who believe in him. Thus, in the very first reference to eternal life in John's narrative, the *terms* are anti-structurally derived from the image of Moses. The same is true in John 6, where the "mannah" "Jews" believed to have been given by Moses enabled some of his people to live only for a while, for eventually "they died" (6:49). In contrast with this "bread from heaven" (6:31), Jesus himself is "the *true* bread from heaven, . . . the bread of God which descends [*katabaino*] from heaven, and gives life to the world" (6:32–33). He *is* "the bread of life," and those who believe in him have *"eternal* life" (6:47–51). The terms applied to Jesus— "bread," "descent," and "life"—all come from the image of Moses. There is much more in John 6, but before we turn to it let us return for a moment to John 3.

In view of the role played by the image of Moses in 3:13–15, we should also see several statements in 3:31–36 as being anti-structurally related to that image. In the earlier statements, Jesus was contrasted with Moses. Here, the narrator formulates the contrast as being between "he who is of the earth," "belongs" to it, and "speaks of it," and "he who comes from above" (*anothen;* cf. vv. 3 and 7) and "bears witness to *what he has seen and heard,"* the one whom *"God has sent"* and who *"utters the words of God."* Moses is not explicitly mentioned, but the key (italicized) terms in what is affirmed about Jesus derive from the image of Moses. And in addition to the anti-structural appropriation and reorientation of these terms, Moses is implicitly subordinated to Jesus when the narrator says that "he who comes from above/from heaven is *above all"* (3:31).

We have had occasion to refer to two anti-structural statements in John 6, one concerning Jesus' having seen the Father (6:46) and the other concerning the contrast between the bread from heaven and the *true* bread from heaven (6:31–32).

However, there are yet other instances of anti-structural thinking and language in this chapter. Indeed, the concluding encounter between Jesus and "Jews" is a showdown over whether or not he is a prophet like Moses. Jesus had performed a number of signs (cf. 6:2–15, 16–25, 26), and he tells "Jews" that they must "believe in him whom God has sent" (6:29), thus appropriating for himself terms from the image of Moses held by his audience. For they respond by saying, "Then what sign do *you* do, that we may see, and believe *you*" (6:30), that is, that God has sent him (6:29). They then refer to the mannah that their ancestors ate in the wilderness, and cite the scriptural passage that says, "He gave them bread from heaven to eat" (6:31). From Jesus' response in 6:32ff., it is apparent that they thought *Moses* had given the mannah, and from the context it is clear that they construed this as a sign that Moses had been sent and was therefore to be believed. For them to believe that Jesus was a prophet like Moses, Jesus would have to perform a sign like Moses'. Jesus' response is anti-structural because he accepts their *terms* but reacts against them by redefining them.

Jesus' anti-structural response is once again comprised of both a negation and an affirmation: "... it was *not Moses* who gave you the bread from heaven; *my Father* gives you the *true* bread from heaven . . . which *descends [katabaino]* from heaven, and gives life *to the world*" (6:32–33). Jesus does not deny that the ancestors ate mannah in the wilderness, as scripture says, but only that it was Moses who gave it. This explicit rejection of beliefs about Moses echoes the implicit rejection of beliefs about his ascent and his seeing God, but it is also related to the statement in 3:14–15 about his lifting up the bronze serpent. For what is believed about Moses' deeds is contrasted with Jesus *himself*, there his being exalted, and here his descent, which was the anti-structural subject of 3:13 (see also the reference to Jesus' ascent in 6:62). And here as there, Jesus himself displaces Moses' deed. There, it is his exaltation that gives eternal life; here, he *is* "the *true* bread from heaven" given by *his* Father, and he *descends from heaven* to give *life to the world*. He *is* "the bread of life" (6:35a), and he has "descended from heaven" to do the will of him who sent him (6:38), namely "that everyone who sees the Son and believes in him should have *eternal life*" (6:40). The "fathers ate mannah in the wilderness, and they died. This is the bread which descends from heaven, that a man may eat of it and not die. I am the living bread which descended from heaven; if any one eats of this bread, he will live forever" (6:49–51b). The anti-structural contrast between Jesus and Moses is in this light further represented in Jesus' opening comments to the "Jews": *"Do not labor for the food which perishes, but for the food which endures to eternal life, which the Son of Man will give to you"* (6:27). Moses' involvement with the "food that perishes" is related to his lifting up of the bronze serpent that preserved life for a time, and Jesus' provision of food "which endures to eternal life" is related to the eternal life made possible by his being lifted up/exalted (3:14–15). But these anti-structural relationships are also found in another episode where Moses is not referred to, although its point of departure is in the Law of Moses, in which Moses is said to have written about Jesus (1:45; 5:46; cf. 2:51 and the allusion to Jacob's ladder). The passage is both anti-structural and related to what we have observed thus far.

The story of the Samaritan woman at Jacob's well (4:1–42) takes place at a plot of land that the patriarch Jacob gave to his son Joseph (Gen. 33:19; 48:22), and the woman claims that Jacob gave her people the well (John 4:12). Jesus comes to the well and asks her to give him a drink. After she questions him about how he, a Jew, can ask her, a Samaritan, for a drink, he responds in typical anti-structural fashion. Playing with the notions of Jacob's *giving* the well and the woman's *giving* him a drink, he says, "If you knew *the gift of God,* and who it is that is saying to you, 'Give me a drink', you would have asked him, and *he would have given you living* water" (4:10). Jesus therefore accepts the terms provided by scripture and by the woman, but he inverts the direction of the giving and contrasts his superior gift with the lesser ones of Jacob and the woman.[30] The implication of superiority is reflected both in her asking Jesus if he is "greater than our father Jacob, who gave us the well . . ." (4:12), and in his response, in which he contrasts the well's water with the 'water' that he has to give: "Everyone who drinks of this water will *thirst again,* but whoever drinks of the water that I shall give him will *never thirst;* the water that I shall give him will become in him a spring of water welling up to *eternal life"* (4:12–14). This response is clearly related to the mannah episode, because

Jesus' "living water" (*hudor zon*) is a special language synonym for his "living bread" (6:51, *ho artos ho zon*). Drinking from Jacob's well, one will "thirst again," just as the ancestors ate the mannah "and died." Drinking from Jesus' "water," one will "never thirst," just as after eating the "true bread from heaven" one will "not die," but will "live forever" (6:48–51). And these contrasts all echo that between the life associated on the one hand with the bronze serpent and on the other with Jesus' exaltation.

Finally, having seen that virtually all of the critical terms in John's characterization of Jesus are anti-structurally derived from the image of Moses, we can return to the anti-structural example with which we began, namely the notion that Jesus' 'kingship' is "not of this world." Some critics have concluded that the image of Moses known by John included the understanding of Moses as a prophet-king different from the traditional notion of a Davidic king.[31] We have found that John's Jesus is a prophet like Moses, yet different primarily because of where he has been sent from, and we have also seen that he is a 'king', yet different for exactly the same reason. Therefore, if the notion of 'king' is part of the image of Moses it, too, will have provided a structural basis for Jesus' anti-structural response to Pilate: "My kingship is *not of this world* . . . For this I was born, and for this I *have come into this world*, to bear witness to the Truth" (18:36–37; cf. 3:33, "God is true").

The idea that Jesus is a "witness" provides a bridge to our next topic of concern, the relationship between Jesus and "the disciples of Moses." However, although we will be shifting our focus, we will still be concerned with the image of Moses, because the Law of Moses which is pivotal in that relationship belongs to the image.[32]

Jesus and the Disciples of Moses

The juridical character of the interaction between characters in John's narrative is abundantly evident, on the one hand in the notion of 'signs' as evidence that is to be believed or disbelieved, and on the other hand in the frequent references to witnesses and testimony, which are also to be believed or disbelieved.[33] Already in the prologue, the Baptist is characterized as a "witness" (1:7–8, 15), and in the opening episode he makes a "confession" while under interrogation by Jewish officials (1:20). And the narrative concludes with Jesus' arrest, two trials, and his execution (18:1–19:37). But as we have seen in our consideration of the social situation and of the laws concerning false prophets, there is much more of a juridical nature in John's narrative, and much of it is anti-structural. Jewish authorities judge Jesus' words and deeds on the basis of the Law of Moses, but John inverts the judgmental process by having Jesus judge them, and by having him turn the Law against them, making both Moses and the Law witnesses on Jesus' behalf. Let us look at the relevant texts.

In John 8:12–19, there is a dialogue between Jesus and "Pharisees" in which they accuse him of bearing false testimony because he "bears witness" to himself (8:12–13). Jesus acknowledges that a law of Moses is at issue, one that maintains that only "the testimony of two men is true" (8:17; cf. Deut. 17:6; 19:15). But while he accepts the terms of his accusers, his response is anti-structural for two reasons. On the one hand, in compliance with the law he offers a second witness: "I bear witness to myself, and the Father who sent me bears witness to me" (12:18). Based on his claim to having been sent by the Father, he anti-structurally contrasts his knowledge with theirs, stating that *he* knows where he has come from and where he is going, but that they do *not*. They "know" neither him nor the Father, for if they knew him they would know the Father also (8:14, 19). His testimony is "true" because of his knowledge of the facts and because of his Father's supporting testimony, which is not further identified in this passage. On the other hand, Jesus therefore also turns the tables on his judges by making his judgment "true" because it is the judgment of both himself and his Father, who sent him (8:16). In their accusation, they are judging falsely because they are judging "according to the flesh" (8:15), that is to say, on the basis of what they 'know', whereas Jesus judges on the basis of what *he* 'knows', which is related to who sent him and whence he has come. As earlier, *Jesus* is the criterion for interpreting the Law, not vice versa, as the "Pharisees" insisted. Two other passages echo the same notions as well as develop some that are left undeveloped here.

In 7:14–29 Jesus again accedes to the Mosaic image when he affirms that his teaching is not his own, but that of the one who sent him (17:16), and this is again related to the audience's thinking that they know him and where he has come from, but do not (7:27–28a). They do not know who sent him, but Jesus does, for he came from him and was sent by him (7:28b–29). In addition, he judges them by claiming that they do not keep the Law given to them by Moses (7:19, 22–23), and that their rejection of him for his healing someone on a sabbath is based on a wrong interpretation of the Law of Moses, which in fact offers a precedent for Jesus' deed on a sabbath. As in 8:15, his judges judge "by appearances," not "with right judgment" (7:19–24).

In 5:30–47, Jesus also affirms the Mosaic premise that if he is bearing witness to himself, his testimony is "not true" (5:31). He claims, however, that in Mosaic terms his judgment is just because he is not seeking his own will, but the will of him who sent him (5:30). In support of this claim, he cites both the testimony of John the Baptist (5:32–35) and the greater testimony of the "works" he does, for these, like Moses' signs, are evidence that the Father has sent him; indeed, they *are* the testimony of his Father (5:36–37a). Then, he once again inverts the tables of judgment by turning scripture against them, first reminding them of Deut. 18:15–19, according to which *they* have never heard the Father's voice, or seen his "form," and then judging that *they* have broken the Law because they do not have the Father's word abiding in them, for they "do not believe him whom he has sent" (5:38). A portion of the passage from Deuteronomy is worth repeating: "I will raise up for them a prophet like you from among their brethren; and I will put my words in his mouth, and he shall speak to them all that I command him. *And whoever will not give heed to my words which he shall speak in my name, I myself will require it of him*" (Deut. 18:18–19). Jesus has presented the credentials of a prophet like Moses, but "Jews" have not believed them. Because they did not "give heed" to the words that God put in Jesus' mouth, they stand indicted by the very Law by which they judged Jesus. And in yet another anti-structural twist, Jesus transforms Moses from being their mediator and intercessor into their *accuser*.[34] Again juxtaposing a negation with an affirmation, Jesus says, "Do *not* think that I shall accuse you to the Father; *it is Moses who accuses you*, on whom you set your hope. If you believed Moses, you would believe me, for he wrote of me. But if you do not believe his writings, how will you believe my words?" (5:45–47). "Jews" "search the scriptures," thinking that in them they have "eternal life," yet the scriptures bear witness to Jesus and "Jews" refuse to come to him that they may "have life" (5:39–40; cf. 1:45). Deuteronomy 18:18–19 leads us to two final passages in which the disciples of Moses wrongly judge Jesus by not following the injunction to heed the words of the one whom God sends. In John 8:31–59, Jesus initiates a dialogue with Jews by saying, "If you continue in my word, you are truly my disciples" (8:31).[35] However, they seek to kill him because his words find no place in them (8:37). They do not understand him because they are not able to "hear" his word (8:43), as God told them to (Deut. 18:15, 19, Greek). Because he tells them the truth, they do not believe him (8:45). He speaks of what he has seen with his Father, but they do what they have heard from their father, Abraham (8:38). Yet they do not do what Abraham did, either, thus proving that neither God nor Abraham is their father. Their father is the devil, who is "the father of lies" (8:39–44). Their disbelief is therefore an act of disobedience that convicts them, and so Jesus concludes, "He who is of God hears the words of God; the reason why you do not hear them is that *you are not of God*" (8:47). They do not know God, but Jesus does (8:55), and those who keep his word will "never see death" (8:51). Thus once again we find John's anti-structural contrasts, inversions, and negations.

The same themes are found in the episode about the good shepherd in John 10.[36] In the opening "figure," Jesus refers to the sheep hearing the shepherd's voice as he calls and leads them out (10:3). They follow him because they know his voice, but they will not follow a stranger because "they do not know the voice of strangers" (10:4–5). In a continuation of Jesus' opening monologue, unbelieving Jews then confront him about whether or not he is the Christ. Jesus responds by saying that he has told them and that still they do not believe. The works he has done in his Father's name bear witness to him, but they do not believe because *they do not belong to his sheep* (10:26). His sheep hear his voice and follow him; and they will have eternal life and never perish (10:27–28). While the good shepherd is here clearly a figure for the prophet like Moses referred to in Deut. 18:15–22, Jesus' words about having life rather than perishing allude to yet other of Moses' words in Deuteronomy, namely in Deut. 30:14–20, which also informs the notion in John 8:37 that Jesus' words "find no place in them." In Deuteronomy 30 Moses tells the people that the word (i.e., the commandment) is in their mouths and in their hearts, and that they can do it (Deut. 30:14). He then tells them that if they obey the commandments and keep them, they shall live, but that if their hearts turn away, and if they will not *hear*, they shall *perish* (30:15–20). Deuteronomy has other concerns than John, because what is at issue there has to do with how Israel will fare when they enter the promised land. Nevertheless, John clearly develops the principles set forth in Deuteronomy 30 and, as we will see in the next chapter, even more extensively than we have found in connection with John 8 and 10. For now, however, it will suffice to observe that as in John 8, the shepherd episode turns the tables on Jesus' detractors by invoking their own norms against them. By virtue of their failure to hear the words of the one whom God has sent, they have convicted themselves, and the disciples of Moses, their intercessor, stand accused by him. The judges become the judged on the basis of the very norms to which they appealed, the words of God communicated through Moses. And this is an anti-structural irony, for those who appealed to Moses in judging Jesus to be a false prophet find Jesus judging them to have failed to hear, believe, and obey the prophet like Moses. But as we have seen, Jesus is the prophet like Moses, yet other and more than he. John uses the everyday language to make his point about those who speak it, but he is also saying something more and something other.

Enough. The evidence is clear. John anti-structurally derives the key terms of his characterization of Jesus from the image of Moses adhered to by the disciples of Moses who are persecuting his people. The sociology of Light begins with the conflict between the disciples of Moses and the disciples of Jesus, and it ends with the sociology of language, in which John's special language proves to be the anti-language of the anti-society comprised of Johannine disciples of Jesus. But there is yet more.

A number of loose ends remain from this as well as from the preceding chapters. Many of these are related to a conceptual system that was intentionally bypassed in Chapter 3, but to which we must now turn in the light of what we have seen in the present chapter about Moses, the Law, and Jesus. The system is one having to do with ancient Jewish images of the feminine personification of God's "Wisdom," which in the Greek is translated by the feminine name *Sophia*. Critics have long recognized the importance of the image of Sophia as an influence on both John's thought and his characterization of Jesus. However, we will approach the role of Sophia's image in John's narrative from a different, sociolinguistic angle and find that his play with her image is anti-structural in a quite surprising way, not least of all because of the relationship between Sophia and Moses. Let us revisit the prologue to John's narrative.

Chapter 5

The Prologue Revisited

Readers familiar with Johannine studies will by now have wondered about the absence of comment on a conceptual system long known to have played a major role in John's characterization of Jesus, a system having to do with the personified Wisdom of God. In a number of Jewish "Wisdom" texts, God's wisdom is personified as a female who was active in creation and subsequently sent to Israel to teach the ways of life and death. Her personification is best represented by the Greek word for 'wisdom', *Sophia*, which is also a feminine name. Although the texts tell different stories about Sophia, John appears to have known a story about her that includes elements from the other ones.[1] Surely, therefore, the system known by John deserved consideration in Chapter 3, where we discussed several other systems. At issue in that discussion was the relationship in John of systems that exist largely independently of one another outside of John. By separating them, we were able to see both the particular character of each of them and the referent blurring effects of John's bringing them together. In fact, we did entertain some aspects of the Sophia system in connection with the Word, which in John assumes several of the functions of Sophia. However, the Sophia system contains much more than these functions, and not least of all concerning Moses. For this reason, it seemed best to defer consideration of Sophia until we had discussed John's anti-structural use of the image of Moses in Chapter 4. As we will see, Sophia became important for John because her story already contained a revisionist view of Moses that was congenial to John's anti-structural endeavor. But John not only used Sophia against Moses, he also contested the Sophia system itself, while at the same time appropriating much of it for his own characterization of Jesus. In this chapter, we will first consider John's use of the image of Moses in the Sophia system, and then we will explore the role of Sophia herself in John's system of characterization.

The Only Son of the Father and the Many Sons of Sophia

Much of what John says about "the Word" in his prologue is said of Sophia in Jewish Wisdom texts. In the course of this chapter, we will be concerned with the relationship among Sophia, the Word, and Jesus, but for our immediate purposes one common feature is important because it pertains to Moses. Although critics differ as to whether the notion of 'the Word' is a substitute for or a synonym of 'Sophia',[2] one Wisdom text affirms of her that she 'dwelt among us', using the same Greek root verb *skenoo* that John uses of the Word's 'dwelling among us' in 1:14.[3] The difference is that while in John the Word "dwelt among us" in the form of Jesus, in some Wisdom texts Sophia 'dwelt among us' in the form of "the Law which Moses commanded us" (Sir. 24:23, Bar. 4:1, on which texts see further below). This contrast between the forms of presence is made explicit in John 1:17, where the narrator says, "For the Law was given through Moses; Grace and Truth came through Jesus Christ." As we saw in the last chapter, *this* contrast is anti-structurally related to another one between the Word's presence as "the only Son [*monogenes*] from the Father" (1:14b) and Moses as a "friend" of God; God is related to Moses as a friend, but He is related to Jesus as the father of an only son. And in the last chapter, we also found both that the next reference to "the only Son," who alone saw God and made him known (1:18), was anti-structurally derived from the notion that Moses saw God, and that this is related to the contrast in 1:17 between the Law that came through Moses and the Grace and Truth that came through Jesus Christ.[4] The notion of Sophia's 'dwelling' among humans is therefore related to John's anti-structural contrast between the "only Son" and Moses. However, in addition to the "only Son's" displacement of Moses, we also have in John a double displacement of Sophia, first in the Word's displacement of her as the one who dwells among humans, and second in the form in which the dwelling occurs. Before we turn to this peculiar adaptation of the image of Sophia, let us return to the contrast between the "only Son" and Moses, for the contrast is found in all four of John's references to "the only Son."

Connections among Sophia, Moses, and Jesus are also evident in the contexts of the two other references to the "only Son" in 3:16 and 18 (cf. vv. 31–36). We have seen that the descent of the Son of Man in 3:13 is related to the anti-Moses statement in 3:14–15, and that the descent is elaborated in 3:16–21 in terms of God's 'giving' and 'sending' his "only Son," and the coming of the Light into the world. Shortly, we will find that 3:13–21 is heavily dependent on the Sophia system, and that it contains the same double displacement of her as in 1:14–18, although without reference to the Law. For now, the point is that the notion of "the only Son from the Father" is *always* found in connection with anti-structural statements about Moses in which the "Son" assumes the role played by Sophia in Jewish wisdom texts. There are two related but separable issues here, one concerning the only Son and Moses, the other concerning the only Son and Sophia. Let us take up the former of these first, in order to see that the notion of the "only Son" is itself anti-structurally related to the image of Moses in the Sophia system. To see this, we have to consider the roles of fathers, mothers, and sons in some Wisdom texts.

One of the many distinctive features of the image of Sophia is that she has metaphorical children. This motif is known from the Jesus tradition prior to John, for Luke 7:35 refers to both the Baptist and "the Son of Man" as "children" (*teknon*) of Sophia.[5] But the earliest evidence of Sophia's "sons" is in the book of Proverbs. In Prov. 1:8 and 6:20, "Solomon" addresses *his* sons and refers to Sophia[6] as their "mother," and in 8:32–36 Sophia addresses her audience as "my sons."[7] In Proverbs, the word 'wisdom' is a proper name, but because the word also maintains its function as an abstract noun it renders Sophia's "sons" as metaphorical sons: They are those who are wise because they have wisdom (Prov. 2:6; 3:19). In addition, "Solomon" is not only Sophia's metaphorical husband, but he is also the son of

King David, and he is himself a king. Later Wisdom texts develop these notions in various ways.

In the Wisdom of Solomon, "Solomon" refers to himself as "the son" of God's "maidservant" (Wis. 9:5), who from the context is none other than Sophia (9:1–4). In this text, therefore, Solomon is now one of Sophia's "sons," not her husband. By implication, moreover, Solomon is also one of God's "sons," for God is the "Father" of all righteous people, and they boast that "God is their Father" (2:16, 18). So in the Wisdom of Solomon, God and Sophia are spouses, and Solomon is one of their "sons." But other sons are probably also implied when the text says that "in every generation she [Sophia] passes into holy souls and makes them friends of God and prophets" (7:27b; cf. v. 14). It will be recalled that in Exod. 33:11 God is said to have spoken to Moses "as a man to his *friend*." According to the Wisdom of Solomon, Sophia "entered the soul" of Moses (10:16; cf. vv. 15–21), "a holy prophet" (11:1), and implicitly made him a friend of God. The text does not explicitly say that Moses was one of Sophia's "sons," but from the context, and from Proverbs and Sirach, in which Sophia is the "mother" of multiple sons (Sir. 4:11; 15:2), Moses can easily be understood as one of Sophia's "sons." He is the one from his generation whom Sophia made "a friend of God" and "a prophet," and he is also the last and climactic of such in the history of Sophia's relations with individuals narrated in Wisdom of Solomon 10–11. In this light, therefore, John's claim that Jesus is "the only Son from the Father," a claim that he only makes in anti-Moses statements, appears to be anti-structurally derived from the notion that Moses was *one* of mother Sophia's "sons." The "only" one is contrasted with the "one of many."

Support for this conclusion comes from another source, and it is all the stronger if in John's knowledge Moses is a prophet-king.[8] In Proverbs and the Wisdom of Solomon, Solomon is King David's son, and in the latter text he is a "son" of both God and Sophia. Outside of these texts, father-and-son language is also related in a significant way to Solomon and David, although Sophia does not play a role. In 2 Sam. 7:12–14, the charter text for the Davidic dynasty, God tells the prophet Nathan to say to David, "When your days are fulfilled and you lie down with your fathers, I will raise up your son after you, who shall come forth from your body, and I will establish his kingdom . . . *I will be his Father, and he shall be my Son.*" Subsequently in Judahite history, every Davidic king became God's metaphorical "son" upon his enthronement. God is therefore the "Father" of a succession of Davidic "sons," just as Sophia is the "mother" of a succession of her "children." John appears to be aware of these parallel traditions because Jesus' being "the *only* Son from the Father" contradicts the Davidic tradition, whose father-and-son language he adopts, just as much as it contradicts the Sophia tradition, whose language of "sons," "children," and "friends" he also adopts. Indeed, he also knows of the notion of a single "prophet" and "king" ("Messiah") who "is coming into the world" (4:19, 25; 6:14–15; 7:31, 40–42, 52; 11:27), but he contradicts it, too, because for him the coming one is "the *only* Son from the Father," who sent him *from heaven,* and his kingship is *"not* of this world" (18:36). For all of these reasons, we must conclude that John's polemically situated insistence on the notion of an "only Son" makes no sense unless it is an anti-structural response to the notion of a plurality of "sons." And because Moses is his principal anti-structural target, and explicitly so in the contexts of his references to "the only Son," John himself is evidence for the understanding of Moses as *one* of Sophia's "sons."

But let us not forget "mother" Sophia, for John's treatment of her is also anti-structural. In John, Jesus is "the only Son," but his "Father" is also his only parent. Mother Sophia is not only absent as a character, but *Jesus* also takes over her roles, including those of enabling people to become both *his* "friends" (15:15) and "children of God" (1:12; 11:52). Moreover, these "children" are "sons of Light" (12:36), the "Light" that is incarnate in Jesus.

Because John's Jesus usurps the role of Mother Sophia, we must now turn to the image of Sophia in order to see what John got from it and what he did with it. The critical question is, How does John get from Moses to Sophia in his anti-structural thinking? His point of departure is from the notion of Moses as one of Sophia's "sons," but John uses this as a base for moving from Moses to Sophia to Jesus.

From Moses to Sophia to Jesus

Critics often say that the descent/ascent schema that John applies to Jesus derives from the notion of Sophia's descent and ascent.[9] There is no question about John's having taken much from the Sophia tradition but, contrary to what is said, the *words* 'ascend' (*anabaino*) and 'descend' (*katabaino*) are *not* used of Sophia in the Jewish Wisdom texts, and only one of them speaks of her 'return' to heaven, and that following an unsuccessful search for a dwelling place, not after being rejected by people among whom she had appeared (1 Enoch 42, on which see further below).[10] Indeed, one of the principal differences between John's story and the Sophia system is that she does *not* return from her dwelling on earth, whereas the Son does return. On the other hand, however, John employs other terminology associated with Sophia's *coming* while making anti-structural statements related to *Moses'* ascent and descent. We therefore return once more to Moses and to a most critical text for our understanding of John's characterization of Jesus.

In Bar. 3:29–4:4 a number of things are said about Sophia that are also said of Jesus in John 3:13–21, which we have found to be anti-structurally related to the image of Moses. But the passage in Baruch is also related to Moses because it is an anti-structural revision of a statement made by Moses himself in Deut. 30:11–20. Let us begin with the relationship between Baruch and John, and then consider their relationships to Deuteronomy.

The passage in Baruch begins with a statement that is clearly related to John 3:13, where Jesus says that "no one has ascended [*anabebeken*, from *anabaino*] into heaven, but he who descended [*katabas*, from *katabaino*] from heaven, the Son of Man." The author of Baruch rhetorically asks, "Who has ascended [*anebe*, from *anabaino*] into heaven and taken/received [*elaben*, from *lambano*] her [Sophia], and brought her down from the clouds" (Bar. 3:29). He then answers his question by saying, "No one knows the way [*ten hodon*] to her, or is concerned about the path to her" (3:31). Baruch is here employing the traditional motif of no one knowing how to find Wisdom (cf. Job 28:12–13, 20–21, 23), but for our purposes what is important is the relationship between what he says and what John says, for both deny that anyone has ascended into heaven and gotten what they were looking for. And in this respect, both agree with Prov. 30:1–3 (Greek) in which a speaker asks, "Who has ascended [*anebe*] into heaven [and learned Sophia] and come down [*katebe*]?" God has to "teach" people Sophia. So while John received the notion and words of 'ascent' and 'descent' from the Moses tradition, he received the *denial* of ascent and descent from the Sophia tradition, which also provided him with the conception, but not the words, for the Son's descent and ascent, which is simply an inversion of the movements associated with Moses. All of this is evident from a comparison of Baruch with John 3, between which there a number of significant relationships that to my knowledge have not previously been observed.

In Baruch, the author moves from saying that "no one knows the way to her" to the claim that God knows her and that he found her by his understanding (3:32; cf. Job 28:23 and Prov. 3:13). Then, after some praise of God (3:32b–35), the author says that having found Sophia, God "*gave* [*edoken*] her to Jacob his servant and to *Israel whom he loved* [*egapameno*]. Afterward she appeared [*ophthe*] on earth and lived among men" (3:36–37; Greek, 3:37–38; cf. Prov. 2:6, God "gives" Sophia, and Prov. 30:3, God "has taught Sophia"). In John, after Jesus denies that anyone had ascended, and after the statement concerning Moses' lifting up the serpent (3:14–15), the narrator says, "For God so *loved* [*egapesen*] *the world* that *he gave* [*edoken*] *his only Son* [*ton huion ton monogene*], that whoever believes in him may have *eternal life*" (3:16). The parallels between this statement and the one in Baruch are even closer when we remember that for John "the world" is synonymous with "the Jews," which in Baruch is represented by "Israel." But the parallels extend yet further when we find Baruch saying of Sophia that "all who hold her fast *will live and those who forsake her will die*" (4:1b), and urging Jacob to "*take/receive* [*epilabou*] her" and "walk toward the shining of her light [*photos*], which is the *glory* [*doxan*] she extends to Jacob" (4:2–3). In John, the narrator says that God "sent" the Son to "save" the world, and that "the *Light* [*phos*] has come into the world and men loved darkness rather than light," indeed, they hated the Light (3:17–21). Those who do evil do not "come to the Light"; those who do, come "to the Light" (3:20–21). To this we must add the conclusion to the narrator's summation: "He who believes in the Son has eternal life; he who does not obey the Son shall not see Life, but the wrath of God rests upon him" (3:36). For John, too, it will be recalled that 'believing' is synonymous with 'receiving' (1:11–12; cf. 3:11). And last, we must note that in Bar. 4:1a Sophia is said to *be* "the book of the command-

ments of God, and the Law that endures forever." We will return to this identification later.

Comparison of Bar. 3:29–4:4 and John 3:11–21 and 31–36
shows that the relationships between them extend beyond the
obvious linguistic and conceptual parallels to the sharing of an
entire story.[11] The story is a simple one: *No one receives what they
seek from God by ascending into heaven, but only as a result of God's
giving it to his people, whom he loves. It appeared on earth and lived
among his people, giving life to those who came to it and received it,
while those who did not do so died.* These linguistic, conceptual, and
narrative relationships enable us to take a step further in our answer to the question of how John moved from Moses to Sophia
to Jesus. John received from the Moses tradition the idea that
Moses and possibly others had ascended into heaven and then
descended, and from the Sophia tradition he received the *denial*
that anyone had ascended into heaven and descended. But
along with this denial he received from the Sophia tradition the
notion that someone, namely Sophia, was given from heaven.

Because the denial is in Baruch part of a revision of a speech
by Moses, our next step forward requires us to consider the relationships among Baruch, John, and Deut. 30:11–20. In the passage from Deuteronomy, Moses admonishes the people about
the "commandment" he has given them, saying, "It is not in
heaven, that you should say, '*Who will ascend* [*anabesetai*] *into
heaven, and bring* [*lempsetai*, from *lambano*] *it to us . . . ?* Neither is
it beyond the sea, that you should say, 'Who will go over the sea
and bring it to us?'" (Deut. 30:11–13). For Deuteronomy's Moses, the "commandment" is present on earth, and it defines the
way to life, while those who turn away from it will perish. Moses presents the people with a choice between life and death,
and he urges them to "choose life" and to love and obey God
(30:14–20). Baruch 3:29–30, which contains both the ascent and
the sea motifs from Deuteronomy, is clearly a reformulation of
Deut. 30:11–13. However, for Moses there was no *need* to ascend
into heaven and receive the commandment, while for Baruch,
like John, no one *has* ascended into heaven to receive Sophia.
For Moses, God commanded him to give the commandment to
Israel, and he did, making it present among the people. For Baruch, God gave Sophia to his people because they could not find
her, and she "*is* the book of the commandments of God, and the

Law that endures forever" (4:1a). For Moses, obedience to the commandment brings life, and disobedience, death, while for Baruch all who hold Sophia fast "will live, and those who forsake her will die" (4:1b). From these relationships, it is evident that although the denial of ascent is known from the Greek translation of Proverbs referred to earlier, John's version of the denial is closest to Baruch's formulation, which is itself a reformulation of Deut. 30:11–20. Let us reserve for later consideration the significant fact that Baruch's reformulation of Moses' speech eliminates Moses and replaces his role with Sophia's. Of more immediate concern is the question of whether or not John was aware of the passage in Deuteronomy independently of the reformulation found in Baruch. If he was, John 3:13 has further anti-Moses implications.

John's independent awareness of Deut. 30:11–20 is indicated by some differences between John and Baruch in which John's differences correspond to some points in Deuteronomy that are not in Baruch. Although Baruch sounds like Deuteronomy when he refers to life and death as the consequences of holding fast to Sophia or forsaking her (4:1b), John phrases matters differently and in terms closer to Deuteronomy when he says, "Whoever believes in him *should not perish [apoletai]* but have eternal life" (3:16). This is then rephrased in 3:17–18: "For God sent the Son into the world, *not to condemn the world, but that the world might be saved* through him. He who believes in him is not condemned; he who does not believe in him is already condemned . . ." Although Deuteronomy, Baruch, and John all cite the positive before the negative, John is closer to Deuteronomy because in both the positive is *intended* for life or living, and in both the negative, "death" or "perishing," are consequences of not "loving" God or "obeying" him (Deut. 30:15–16, 19–20; cf. 5:33).[12] Terminologically, the word 'perish' [*apollumi*] appears in John 3:16 and Deut. 30:18, but not in Baruch, and 'loving' and 'obeying' are used of the Son in 3:19 and 3:36, and of God in Deut. 30:16 and 20, and in both cases life is the consequence of such behavior. Neither verb is in Baruch's passage. And last, John 3:36b, "he who does not *obey* the Son shall not see *life,* but *the wrath of God* rests upon him," sounds very much like a condensation of Deut. 30:16–18a, "If you *obey* the commandments . . . you *shall live* . . . If your heart turns away . . . you *shall perish* [*apoleisthe*]."

118

From these relationships between John and Deuteronomy, it appears that John was aware of the Deuteronomic text that Baruch or others revised. This means that John knew not only of the Sophia tradition's denial of ascent into heaven, but also of Moses' denial of the *need* to ascend into heaven. And for this reason, John's anti-Moses claim that no one *has* ascended into heaven is reinforced by his turning Moses' own words against those who believed in *Moses'* ascent and descent. On the other hand, the relationships between the passages in Baruch and John also make it clear that John's use of the story of Sophia cannot be separated from his focus on the image of Moses. We can only make sense of his use of that story by understanding it as a part of his anti-structural response to the image of Moses adhered to by the disciples of Moses. But it is further evident that once John adopted the story of Sophia for his anti-Moses purposes, the story also provided him with the essentials of both the plot of his own story and the structure of its system of characterization. The relationship among the Father, his only Son, and those who do or do not receive him, and therefore do or do not receive life, is anti-structurally derived from the story of Sophia. But that story, at least in its Baruchian form, is itself an anti-structural revision of the story of Moses, because God's direct giving of Sophia *as* the Law replaces the notion of God's sending of Moses *with* the Law. What is more, John's Jesus also anti-structurally relates to the Sophia story because Jesus displaces Sophia both as the one who was given from heaven, and as the Law of Moses, which two Wisdom texts identify as the form of her presence in Israel/the world (Bar. 4:1a; Sir. 24:23). God gives his only Son, *not* Sophia, and this gift is Jesus, *not* the Law of Moses. And the latter displacement conforms to what John says in his prologue: "For the Law was given [*edothe*] through Moses; Grace and Truth came through Jesus Christ," who is the only Son, who in turn is the form of the Word's 'dwelling' in the world (1:17).

Let us turn now to other Wisdom texts in order to see how their stories of Sophia further contribute to John's characterization of Jesus.

Sophia and John's Characterization of Jesus
Other Wisdom texts either elaborate on elements of the story seen in Baruch or add features to it. While it is unclear whether

John knew all of these texts or a more developed story of Sophia than any one of them represents, his own narrative reflects features of them all. We begin with Sirach 24 which, like Proverbs 8, is in the first person singular speech of Sophia herself (cf. the third-person descriptions of Sophia in Sirach 1). Sirach develops some points found in Baruch's story, but he also has other points that are developed further in Proverbs and yet other texts.

Critics often note that Sophia's use of the first person in Sirach and Proverbs is related to Jesus' use of the first person in John, not only grammatically but also materially, for they both speak about themselves. Surely, this is a major contribution of the story of Sophia to John's characterization of Jesus. However, we must also note a significant difference, namely that Sophia does not speak in anti-language the way Jesus does. Although personified Sophia is a metaphor for something else, either or both God's wisdom or the Law, she speaks in everyday language. For this reason, John's Jesus is anti-structurally related to Sophia in two ways, first because he displaces her from her roles in the stories about her, and second because *he* speaks in anti-language. Both points should be kept in mind as we review the stories of Sophia in Sirach and Proverbs, and in the Wisdom of Solomon as well, although she does not speak in the first person in that text.

Sophia's first-person discourse in Sirach 24 is also in the past tense because she is reciting her biography. She begins at a point in time prior to the beginning of her story in Baruch, who only says that she was originally in heaven before God gave her to Israel. In Sirach, she claims to have "come forth [*exelthon*] from the mouth of the Most High," dwelling (*kateskenosa*) in high places and traveling around seeking a resting place below in which she might lodge (24:3–7). Her search ended when the creator of all things assigned her a place for her "tent" (*skene*), saying: "Make your dwelling [*kataskenoson;* literally, 'set up your tent'] in Jacob, and in Israel receive your inheritance" (24:8; cf. 1:10). Sophia then backtracks in time by noting that "from eternity, in the beginning [*ap' arches*] he created me, and for eternity I shall not cease to exist" (24:9; cf. 1:1, 4, 9). Then, returning to the time of her resting place in Zion/Jerusalem (24:10–12), she proceeds to describe her growth there, using metaphors of trees and a vine (24:13–17; cf. Prov. 3:18, a "tree of life"), and concludes with a summons to those who "desire" her to "come" to her and "eat" their fill of her produce and "drink" her, which she elaborates with the synonyms of 'obeying' her and 'working' (*ergazomenoi*) with her help (24:19–22). The narrator concludes along the lines of Bar. 4:1a, by saying, "All this is the book of the covenant of the Most High God, *the Law which Moses commanded us*" (24:23).

Parallels between Sirach and John are abundant. For example, 'coming' to Sophia, 'eating' and 'drinking' her, and 'working' with her all appear in connection with Jesus in John 6:25–51, which we have found to be part of John's anti-structural response to the image of Moses. But especially suggestive are some negative statements in John 6 which are anti-structurally opposed to things said by Sophia in Sirach. Whereas Sophia says that those who "come" to her and "eat" her "will hunger for more," and that those who "drink" her "will thirst for more" (24:21), Jesus says, "he who comes to me shall *not* hunger, and he who believes in me shall *never* thirst" (6:35; cf. v. 27 and 4:13–14). Similarly, whereas Sophia exhorts those who "desire" her to "come" to her (Sir. 24:19), Jesus says, "*No one can come to me unless the Father who sent me draws him*" (6:44; cf. v. 45).[13] Also, the notion of 'working' with Sophia and Jesus appears in Sir. 24:22b and John 6:27; and Sir. 24:22a, "Whoever obeys me / will not be put to shame," sounds very much like John 6:37, "him who comes to me / I will not cast out" (cf. John 3:36). In both cases, Jesus anti-structurally displaces Sophia.

Viewed individually, these parallels could be coincidental, but viewed collectively, and in the light of the numerous other traces of Sophia material in John, a coincidence is highly unlikely. And it is all the more unlikely because, as in John 3, John employs the Sophia material in an anti-Moses context. John is reacting against both Moses and Sophia, and if he knows of the Wisdom identification of Sophia with the Law, Jesus' revision of the interpretation of the Law in 6:31–33 suggests that "the food which perishes" (6:27), which one should not labor for, is both the Law as the disciples of Moses understood it, and Sophia as the Wisdom tradition understood "her." And so once again we find echoes of the contrast made in John 1:17 between what came through Moses and what came through Jesus.

More significant than these parallels are two others. The first concerns Sophia's claim that she "made her dwelling," or "set up her tent" (*kataskenoson*) in Jacob/Israel (24:8). It has long been recognized that this is a primary part of the evidence for John's use of the Sophia traditions, for in John 1:14 he employs the same root verb in saying that "the Word became flesh and *dwelt* [*eskenosen*] among us, full of Grace and Truth." But it has also been seen that Sophia's dwelling in Jacob/Israel, her "inheritance," is related to the Light's coming "to his own home" and to "his own people" (John 1:11–12), and that "the Word" is related to Sophia's 'coming forth *from the mouth* of the Most High' (Sir. 24:3). And John's claim that some "beheld" the glory of the Word is likewise related to Baruch's claim that Sophia "appeared" (or "was seen," *ophthe*) on earth and was Israel's "glory" (Bar. 3:37; 4:2). We have seen, too, that because Sophia's appearance was for some in the form of the Law given through Moses (cf. John 1:17), the anti-structural response to Moses in 1:14–18 also responds anti-structurally to Sophia/the Law. Jesus is superior to Moses, who did not see God but only delivered the Law, and he is superior to the Law because as the incarnate Word he has displaced it, just as he has displaced Sophia who, like the Son, metaphorically came directly from God, but who, unlike the Son, was only a metaphor for God's wisdom, not God incarnate.

The second important parallel is also related to the prologue. In Sir. 24:9, Sophia says, "From eternity, in the beginning [*ap' arches*], he created me, and for eternity I shall not cease to exist" (cf. Bar. 4:1a, "the Law that endures forever"). On the one hand, this statement begins at the same point as John 1:1, which says, "In the beginning [*en arche*] was the Word, and the Word was with God." Proverbs, too, thinks of Sophia as having been with God from the beginning (contrast Bar. 3:32, 36, where God had to find her before he could send her, and Job 28:12–13, 20–28, where God found her when others could not), but none of the Wisdom texts identifies Sophia with God like John identifies the Word with God: "and the Word *was* God." Nevertheless, despite this anti-structural, anti-language identification, John has derived from the Sophia tradition the notion of the Word being with God *from the beginning*. On the other hand, Sir. 24:9, like Prov. 8:22–31, has Sophia claim that she was created by

God. In the words of Proverbs, Sophia says, "The Lord created me at the beginning of his work, the first of his acts of old . . . at the first, before the beginning of the earth . . . then I was beside him like a master workman" (8:22–23, 30a; cf. 3:19 and Wis. 8:3, "her noble birth"). Sophia then concludes by addressing her "sons" with words echoed in Baruch: "For he who finds me finds life and obtains favor from the Lord; but he who misses me injures himself; *all who hate me love death*" (Prov. 8:35–36; cf. 3:13, 18, and John 3:20, 36). Apart from the obvious parallels to John (the 'beginning', 'love' and 'hate', 'life' and 'death'), two new points of contact emerge. First, in Proverbs Sophia is active in creation, as are the Word and the Light in John 1:2 and 10. Second, in Proverbs and Sirach Sophia was created by God. Both points require comment.

The first point clearly shows that in John the Word/Light has displaced Sophia's role in creation, and this displacement is even more evident from another Wisdom text we will entertain in a moment. The second point is more immediately pertinent because, whereas for John "the Word *was* God," Sophia was created by God, "the first of his acts of old," and therefore, in effect, she is the first-born of creation (cf. Sir. 1:4).[14] Nevertheless, despite this obvious difference between John's "Word" and Sophia, a trace of Sophia is found in Jesus' references to his resumption of the "glory" that he had with his Father *"before the world was made"* (17:5), *"before the foundation of the world"* (17:24). We must remember, however, that this is the "glory" of the Word, which became flesh in Jesus and manifested *its* "glory" in him "as of the only Son from the Father." Jesus' words in 17:5, 24 are therefore the words of the Word, and for this reason they lead us back to the Word's displacement of Sophia "from the beginning," as well as in creation.

But it is also the case, as we have seen, that as the only Son *Jesus* displaces Sophia in the form of her "dwelling" in the world, whether in the form of a female to be met on the street, however metaphorically, as in Proverbs 1–8, or in the form of the Law, as in Baruch and Sirach. As the form of the Word's dwelling in the world, the "only Son" therefore also displaces the first-born of creation who subsequently came into the world. Jesus' being "the only Son from the Father" thus stands in antistructural contrast not only with Moses as one of Sophia's "sons," but also with Sophia herself as the first-born of creation. Because of the unity, indeed, the identity John ultimately posits between the Father and his only Son, his conception of their relations is vastly more complicated than in Paul, whose own formulation of it is much more straightforward. For in Paul, Jesus is the human form of the first-born Son of God, whose task it is to transform all believers into the form of the sons of God, so that all of God's children can be with the Father in the kingdom of God.[15] John is not Paul, of course, but the comparison is of interest because John's notion of the *"only* Son" is as strategically significant for him as Paul's notion of the *"first-born* Son" is for him. Both qualifications of "Son" are bound up with contrasts that are fundamental for each of them, in Paul, between the first and others to come; in John, between the only one and what others believe to be many, whether as the first (Sophia) or as members of a succession (Sophia's "children"). John's qualifier of "only" is different from Paul's "first" because the "only" is anti-structurally derived from John's social opposites and stands opposed to them.

Finally, speaking of oppositions recalls another statement in Sirach. Although it is not related to Sophia, it does suggest how the Wisdom tradition contributed to John's famous dualities. In Sir. 33:14–15, the speaker says, "Good is the opposite of evil, and life the opposite of death; so the sinner is the opposite of the godly. *Look upon all the works of the Most High; they likewise are in pairs, one the opposite of the other.*"

Yet another Wisdom text, the Wisdom of Solomon, presents a story of Sophia that is both similar to and different from the stories in Baruch, Sirach, and Proverbs. The principal difference is that she does not come to dwell among the people of Israel, but is "given" to individuals, either by passing into holy souls, making them "friends of God and prophets" (7:27b; 10:16), or by working with or through them (10:1–11:1). As noted earlier, too, she "entered the soul" of Moses, but she was also responsible for the things he did, as with the "wonders and signs" he employed against Pharaoh (10:16; 11:1). Indeed, *she* "delivered" the people from their oppressors (10:15). Related to the absence of her "dwelling" among the people is the fact that when she is not present in individual souls, or possibly even when she is in them, she is with God (8:3; 9:4, 9–10, 17). In the

Wisdom of Solomon, therefore, Sophia is not the Law of Moses, but only a slightly veiled representation of "wisdom" as insight and knowledge which is given to individuals directly from heaven. Nevertheless, she is still related to Moses because in the survey of her activities in history in 10:1–11:1 he is the last one into whom she entered. As in Proverbs, the Law is not mentioned in connection with Sophia, but unlike Proverbs Moses is the climax to her reported interventions into history. However, because Sophia is the one who acted through Moses, the Wisdom of Solomon represents another revision of the image of Moses besides the one seen in Baruch and Sirach, where she is the Law. In both cases, the role of Moses is devalued by the role played by Sophia.

The similarities between the Wisdom of Solomon and the other Wisdom texts we have been considering also disclose differences that are pertinent to John's use of the Sophia tradition. As in Sirach and Proverbs, the Sophia of the Wisdom of Solomon is active in the process of creation. However, the role she plays in creation in this text is much closer to John than the creative role ascribed to her in these other texts. Indeed, she plays the role that John attributes to the Word and the Light in 1:4 and 10. For she is now the "fashioner of all things" (7:22; 8:6), and an "initiate in the knowledge of God [cf. John 1:18], and an associate in his works" (8:4). What is more, "Solomon" addresses God as the one "who hast made all things by thy word [*logon*], and by thy wisdom [*sophia*] hast formed man" (9:1), rendering as synonymous the words 'wisdom' and 'word', and thereby providing a bridge from Sophia to "the Word" in John 1. Other attributes of Sophia in the Wisdom of Solomon are also clearly related to John's statements about "the Word." She is "a pure emanation of the *glory* [*doxes*] of the Almighty" (7:25), she sits on the throne of God's *glory* (*doxes*; 9:10), and she is a reflection of "eternal *Light*" (*photos*; 7:26). And like John, this text contrasts Light with the light of day: "Compared with the light she is found to be superior, for it is succeeded by the night" (7:29–30).

Also, like Baruch and John, Wisdom's Sophia is not something that can be sought and found, but must be 'given' by God (Wis. 8:18, 21; 9:17). "Solomon" appeals to God to "give" him the Sophia that sits by his throne (9:4), to "send her forth from thy holy heavens, and from the throne of thy glory send her"

(9:10; cf v. 17, where "Sophia" is also synonymous with "thy holy spirit"). 'Giving' and 'sending' are of course key terms in John 3:16–17, and like the Light that *came* into the world (3:19), Sophia 'comes from God' (Wis. 9:6). And last, related to John's reference to Jacob's ladder in 1:51, to 'seeing' the kingdom of God in 3:3, 5, and to Jesus' 'telling' heavenly things in 3:12 (cf. 3:32), Wisdom's Sophia "showed him [Jacob] the kingdom of God, and gave him knowledge of angels [or holy things]" (10:10; cf. John 1:18).

To conclude our survey of Wisdom texts, we come to the most idiosyncratic of them all, 1 Enoch 42:1–2, with which we began the survey. The text reads: "Sophia found no place where she could dwell, and her dwelling place was in heaven. Sophia went out in order to dwell among the sons of men, but did not find a dwelling; Sophia returned to her place and took her seat in the midst of angels."[16] In view of what we have seen of Sophia, this statement appears to be an anti-structural denial of what is affirmed in Sirach about her seeking a resting place and being given a "dwelling" in Israel as "the Law which Moses commanded us" (Sir. 24:7–8, 23). Usually, critics see 1 Enoch 42 as reflecting the rejection of Sophia along the lines of Prov. 1:20–33 (cf. 8:35–36), where people "hate knowledge," "refuse to listen," and otherwise ignore her "counsel."[17] However, because 1 Enoch 42 is a story of Sophia's failure to find a dwelling place, its difference from Sirach's notion of Sophia's dwelling in Israel in the form of the Law is much more pertinent than any supposed links to Proverbs. The statement in 1 Enoch says nothing about a descent or an ascent, let alone about a time when Sophia was present on earth where she could be accepted or rejected. All it says is that she sought a dwelling place among men but could not find one. On the other hand, in John the Word, like Sophia in Sirach, *did* find a dwelling, and it was in the form of the person of Jesus. For all of these reasons, 1 Enoch 42 has nothing to do with John. But Proverbs does.

In Proverbs 1–8, Sophia simply appears on the street and addresses those around her. She is clearly a metaphor for 'insight' and 'understanding', and it is as such that God "gives" her to people (Prov. 2:1–8). It is in this sense, too, that she is something that can be 'found' or 'gotten' (3:13; 4:5–6). In Proverb's personification of Wisdom, she is 'found' because she presents herself to people as a good woman whose call to them is contrasted with the call of a harlot. However, her call is rejected by some and received by others, with the consequences respectively of death and life (cf. 1:20–33; 2:16–19; 7:1–27; 8:35–36). The opposed forms of consequences are found in other Wisdom texts, but the opposed forms of reception and rejection of Sophia's call to people are only found in John's system of characterization. But as we have observed in connection with the other Wisdom texts, Jesus displaces Sophia by taking her place. Like her, he, as the Word, is active in creation and later comes, as Jesus, to his people to enable them to find life in him, although some hate him and find death. Unlike her, on the other hand, the form of the Word's presence is that of one known to have been a historical human being, and he relates to other human beings who are concrete persons, not metaphorical puppets, as in Proverbs. In John, therefore, Sophia is historicized by being displaced by a human being, and she is politicized by this human being's conflict with the political establishment. And it is through this conflict that the differences between "Jesus" and Sophia are both anti-structural and a fundamental part of John's anti-language. We conclude with some reflections on these differences.

John's Anti-Structural Use of the Image of Sophia

We need not summarize all of the evidence we have seen of John's use of the image of Sophia. *That* he used the image is incontestable. The question is, *how* did he use it, and what effects did his use have on his anti-language characterization of Jesus? Because differences are best seen when measured against similarities, we can take our point of departure from a chart that maps things said about Moses, Sophia, and Jesus. The chart

	Heaven			Earth
1. —	—	Sophia		addresses people directly[18]
2. God	sent	Moses		to people, *with* Law[19]
3. God + Sophia	gave	Sophia		to people, *as* Law[20]
4. God + Sophia	assigned	Sophia		a dwelling place *as* Law[21]
5. Sophia	entered	—		Moses' soul[22]
6. Word = God	became flesh	—		dwelling *as* Jesus[23]
7. God/Father	sent/gave	his only		Son Jesus, to his people[24]

does not represent the roles of Sophia and the Word/Light in creation because the relationships are self-evident. Rather, it focuses on the plot that we first observed in Baruch 3–4 and John 3.

Let us proceed by reviewing some of our previous observations about the image of Sophia and by relating them to the chart.

1. In three of the Wisdom texts, Sophia's interaction with Israel is associated with the Law (Baruch, Sirach) and/or Moses (Wisdom of Solomon, Sirach). The biblical understanding that God sent Moses to Israel and through him gave them the Law is in Baruch and Sirach interpreted in terms of Sophia being given/assigned a dwelling place *as* the Law, which is the form of her presence in Israel. Sophia displaces Moses because she is now both the one who was sent and the Law that was given. Similarly, the Wisdom of Solomon also displaces Moses by having Sophia be the agent operative in his deeds. The Wisdom tradition known to John therefore already contains a revisionist, anti-structural view of Moses.[25] John found this revisionist view congenial to his own reaction to the image of Moses held by the disciples of Moses who used that image as a basis for their rejection of John's people. John therefore adopts features of the Sophia stories found in Baruch and Sirach and uses them as part of his anti-structural response to the image of Moses: The "Son" is sent and *he* is the presence of the "Father."

2. The Sophia tradition knows of both a mother/child system and a Father/Son system. John selects the latter in connection with his anti-structural substitution of the notion of Jesus as "the only Son from the Father" for the notion of Moses as one of Sophia's sons. But because the "only Son" is a metaphor for the Word in its incarnation, and because the Word displaces Sophia, the "only Son" also displaces Sophia as the first-born of creation.

3. In John 3, John anti-structurally derives the notion of the Son of Man's descent and ascent from the tradition of Moses' ascent and descent. However, he also derives from the Wisdom tradition's revision of the image of Moses both its denial that human ascent into heaven could lead to the acquisition of Sophia and the notion that Sophia is only given/sent to Israel from heaven. Consequently, just as Sophia is superior to Moses, so is

the Son superior to both him and Sophia, because the Son displaces both of them.

4. Having adopted the Sophia system in order to support his contrast between Jesus and Moses, John further displaces *her* with the "Word" and transfers to the Word the Sophia motifs of Light, of being with God in heaven from the beginning, of being active in creation, and of being sent/given to Israel, where she dwelled and among whom she made "friends" and "children of God." Thus, just as "Jesus" assumes the role of Moses in the image of Moses, the Word assumes the role of Sophia in the Sophia system, with all of the modifications we have observed. The point is that the image and the system are the bases for the modifications that result in John's system of characterization and in the plot of his story.[26]

5. John's modifications are represented in two principal areas of difference between Sophia and John's "Word." The first has to do with the relationship between them and God, and the second with the relationship between them and the forms of their presence in Israel. In the former, whereas God and Sophia are distinct characters, namely as male and female, the Word and God (and the Light, etc.) are *identical*. In the latter, whereas Sophia either entered holy souls or received a dwelling place as the Law, the Word/God/Light became flesh and dwelled in Israel as Jesus of Nazareth. The Word is therefore anti-structurally contrasted with Sophia, because on the one hand the bipartite structure of her relationship with God is erased, while on the other hand the Word become flesh displaces her dwelling as the Law. To be sure, there is in John a temporary separation of the Word from its fleshly form, as we have observed in the metaphors of Father and Son. But the separation is not only temporary, for unlike Sophia the Son returns whence he came, but it is also undercut by John's insistence that the Father and the Son are "one." Despite the lack of conceptual clarity in John's understanding of this unity, it clearly represents a contrast with the Sophia system, for in John both God and the Word and the Word and Jesus are one, not two or three, although given the limitations of everyday language it is necessary to speak of them as distinct. Indeed, as we found in our reflections on the prologue to John, the unity of God and the Word, and of the Word and Jesus, results in the referent blurring characteristic of John's

special use of language in the prologue and in his merging of multiple conceptual systems (see Chapter 3). To be different from what he rejected, John had to erase difference within that which he affirmed.

The temporary nature of the distinction between Father and Son introduces another, related difference between the Sophia system and John's use of it. Unlike Sophia's dwelling in Israel as "the Law that endures forever" (Bar. 4:1), Jesus' presence as the Word's dwelling place in Israel is only temporary; he not only dies, but the Word that was incarnate in him returns to its original "place." But this leads us to yet another anti-structural contrast, for after Jesus' death and the Word's return there remains a presence that is the functional equivalent of the Law, namely the book of signs known as the Gospel of John. This book is the narrative simulacrum of the presence of the Word, because "belief" in what is in it produces the same effect of "eternal life" that was produced by "belief" in Jesus (John 17:20–21; 19:35; 20:29–31). For John, there is no functional difference between the signs as Jesus performed them and those signs as narrated in John's book. But even this narrative presence is only temporary, because believers will eventually be with "Jesus" (12:32; 13:36; 14:1–3,19, 23, 28; 17:24).

6. The combination of John's notions of unity and of the temporary nature of the Word's presence leads to another aspect of John's use of the Sophia system. We have observed that this system's plot of sending and dwelling provided an underlying unity to his merger of several different conceptual systems. However, the plot of sending and dwelling lacks John's distinctive emphasis on descent and *ascent*, sending and *returning*.[27] Ascent, descent, and return are not derived from the Sophia system. They are anti-structural responses to it because the coming and the going are in the service of John's notion of unity. The going erases the difference in the Other that was created by the coming. But the going also has a further anti-structural role, for it establishes the temporary nature of the Other's presence. There is for John no permanent dwelling of the Other in the world because life in the world is a thing to be hated and endured. Sophia and the Law are agents of life *in* the world, whereas for John eternal life is not of this world. Here we can clearly see the impact of the social history of John's people, a

history that led to the polarization of the Other and the Same, but also to the preference for unity within the Other over difference both between the Other and the Same and within the Same.

7. Finally, the conceptual unity the Sophia system provides to John's narrative is also anti-structurally deconstructed. While John adopts and modifies the plot of the story of Sophia, his displacement of the character Sophia entails a deconstruction of the system's characterization of her. That Sophia *is* the "Word" is not the same as John's notion that the Word *was* God, for in the Sophia system the names "Sophia" and the "Word" are transparent metaphors for 'wisdom', 'knowledge', and 'understanding', and for the message that communicates them. Similarly, that she is "Light" and permanently reflects the glory of God, and that she gives life, are also metaphors for the cognitive and moral 'illumination' that leads to the good life. John systematically deconstructs this unified metaphorical conception by separating the Word and Light systems, then mapping them onto one another and supplementing them with other systems like those of the Father and the Son, the descending and ascending of the Son of Man, and the prophet/Messiah who is coming into the world. The result of these multiple overlays of separate systems is the blurring not only of their individual referents, but also of their collective reference, which in turn results in John's image of the unity of the Other. All that remains from the Sophia system with any clarity of reference is the minimal and, for John, incomplete structure of its plot.

John's story about Jesus is in the final analysis doubly anti-structural, for on the one hand it is a reaction to the story of Moses by which his opponents lived, while on the other hand it is a reaction to the story of Sophia which was itself a revision of the story of Moses.[28] Because John uses the revision against his opponents, it is unlikely that they are the ones who created it. Whether or not they, or even John's people, knew of the revision is unclear, although we do know from the several Sophia stories that knowledge of the Sophia tradition was widespread, and not least of all in certain Christian circles, where "Jesus" also displaced Sophia.[29] However, none of the Christian appropriations reflect the systematic knowledge of the Sophia tradition that we find in John. If the Christian appropriations were known to him, they may have provided him with a basis for his own independent appropriation and revision of the Sophia tradition. But the historical picture remains unclear. What is clear is that the story John told his people about Jesus replaces for him both the story of Moses and the story of Sophia, and his story goes far beyond what other "Christians" did with Sophia, in large part because John's focus was on the story of Moses, which was pivotal in his peoples' conflict with the disciples of Moses.

Conclusion

At the end of the introductory chapter I noted that the everyday language statement that 'God loved the world and sent his Son to give it life' was in fact a special language statement because the terms 'God', the 'world', the 'Son', and 'life' do not for John mean what they mean in everyday language. It is only appropriate to conclude that the same is true of the statement in John 20:31, that "these [signs] are written that you may believe that Jesus is the Christ, the Son of God, and that believing you may have life in his name." Jesus' 'signs' are not signs in the everyday Mosaic sense, 'belief' does not mean what it means in everyday language. Jesus is not what he is perceived to be, and 'Christ', 'Son of God', and 'life' do not mean what they mean in everyday language. As throughout John's narrative, special language meanings are encoded in the words of everyday language.

Notes

Introduction

1. The distinction between everyday language and a special language derived from it was introduced by Herbert Leroy in his *Rätsel und Missverständnis: Ein Beitrag zur Formgeschichte des Johannesevangeliums*, Bonner Biblische Beiträge 30 (Bonn: Peter Hanstein, 1968). See 21–25 and 157–60 for discussion and literature. Leroy's distinction has found considerable acceptance, but his form-critical approach to the riddle-like character of instances of multiple meanings has not. Although Wayne A. Meeks did not employ the distinction between special and everyday language, he independently made a number of related sociolinguistic observations in his "The Man from Heaven in Johannine Sectarianism," *JBL* 91 (1972) 44–72, where he acknowledges his agreement with Leroy. For both of them, John's peculiar use of language is understood in terms of its opposition to the language of a Jewish community that had persecuted his people. Both of their studies were limited in scope, however, because Leroy concentrated on instances of multiple meanings and Meeks on the mythological language of descent and ascent. Nevertheless, their sense that the phenomena they studied were part of a wider linguistic phenomenon related to the conflict between communities marks a distinct advance in the understanding of Johannine language. Whereas critics usually speak of different levels of meaning, such as literal and spiritual, Leroy and Meeks placed the question of meaning in a social context of opposing linguistic usage. Independently of them, Bruce J. Malina added another dimension to the linguistic issue in his "The Gospel of John in Sociolinguistic Perspective," *Center for Hermeneutical Studies*, Colloquy 48 (Berkeley: Center for Hermeneutical Studies, 1985). In this again somewhat limitedly focused

study, Malina introduced the categories of anti-languages and anti-societies developed by the sociolinguist M. A. K. Halliday in his *Language as Social Semiotic: The Social Interpretation of Language and Meaning* (London: Edward Arnold, 1978), while also relating these categories to anthropologist Mary Douglas's grid-group theory of social identification. See, e.g., Mary Douglas, *Natural Symbols: Explorations in Cosmology* (New York: Vintage, 1973), 77–92, and for further discussion of and literature on the theory, see Jerome H. Neyrey, S.J., *An Ideology of Revolt: John's Christology in Social Scientific Perspective* (Philadelphia: Fortress Press, 1988). Neyrey does not take up the notion of anti-language, although he does move from the social to linguistic matters, which he deals with in conceptual terms, e.g., confessions, dualisms, and dichotomies. The importance of the notion of anti-language is that it makes clear what Leroy and Meeks suspected, namely that John's special language is the anti-language of an anti-society, on which see further above and also Chapter 4. It should also be noted that already at the turn of the century William Wrede anticipated much of what recent critics have observed about the social determination of John's peculiar use of language, and not least of all my own concern with the relationships among language, characterization, and social context. See Wrede, "Charakter und Tendenz des Johannesevangeliums," in his *Vorträge und Studien* (Tübingen: Mohr, 1907), 178–231, and his chapter on John in *The Messianic Secret*, trans. J. C. G. Grieg (Greenwood, S.C.: Attic, 1971), 181–207, which was first published in 1901. Also pertinent is Takashi Onuki's *Gemeinde und Welt im Johannesevangelium: Ein Beitrag zur Frage nach der theologischen und pragmatischen Funktion des johanneischen "Dualismus,"* WMANT 56 (Neukirchen-Vluyn: Neukirchener Verlag, 1984). Onuki sees John's dualism as a product of a "boundary language" ("*Grenzsprache*") which emerged in the midst of several linguistic fields. He was aware of Leroy's sociologically oriented contribution, but he saw his own concerns as having to do with the dualistic motifs in their history-of-religions context (e.g., 26–28). Unfortunately, this obscured the significance of the contrast between special and everyday language, which places so-called dualism in a bipolar social context. Birger Olsson, *Structure and Meaning in the Fourth Gospel: A Text-Linguistic Analysis of John 2:1–11 and 4:1–42*, ConBib, NT Series 6 (Lund: Gleerup, 1974), also cites with approval Leroy's notion of a special language, although his own linguistic orientation is to European "text-linguistics," which lacks a social dimension (see 1–17).

2. The literature is considerable, especially on dualism and symbolism, which are usually dealt with in terms of the religious history of symbols and of dualistic pairs. For this reason only a few references will be given. The following items are presented in chronological order,

beginning with what appears to have been an awakening to peculiarities of Johannine language in the 1940s. A foundation of sorts is in the work of Rudolf Bultmann, whose commentary on John, which first appeared in 1941, contains numerous and still valuable linguistic and tropic insights: *The Gospel of John: A Commentary*, trans. G. R. Beasley-Murray et al. (Philadelphia: Westminster, 1971). Further linguistic insights abound in his section on John in his *Theology of the New Testament*, vol. 2, trans. K. Grobel (New York: Scribner's, 1955), which appeared in its original German edition between 1948 and 1953. The remaining bibliography should be consulted for further literature: F. W. Gingrich, "Ambiguity of Word Meaning in John's Gospel," *Classical Weekly* 37 (1943) 77; O. Cullmann, "Der johanneische Gebrauch doppeldeütiger Ausdrücke als Schlüssel zum Verständnis des vierten Evangeliums," *TheolZeit* 4 (1948) 360–72; Leroy, *Rätsel und Missverständnis*; David W. Wead, *The Literary Devices in John's Gospel* (Basel: Reinhardt, 1970); George W. MacRae, "Theology and Irony in the Fourth Gospel," in *The Word in the World*, ed. R. J. Clifford and G. W. MacRae (Weston: Weston College, 1973), 83–96; Kim E. Dewey, "*Paroimiai* in the Gospel of John," *Semeia* 17 (1980) 81–99; X. Leon Dufour, "Towards a Symbolic Reading of the Fourth Gospel," *NTS* 27 (1981) 439–56; C. K. Barrett, "Symbol," and "Paradox and Dualism," in Barrett, *Essays on John* (Philadelphia: Westminster, 1982), 65–79, 98–115; Donald A. Carson, "Understanding Misunderstandings in the Fourth Gospel," *Tyndale Bulletin* 33 (1982) 59–91; R. Alan Culpepper, *Anatomy of the Fourth Gospel: A Study in Literary Design* (Philadelphia: Fortress Press, 1983); E. Richard, "Expressions of Double Meaning and Their Function in the Gospel of John," *NTS* 31 (1985) 96–112; Paul D. Duke, *Irony in the Fourth Gospel* (Atlanta: John Knox, 1985); Gail R. O'Day, *Revelation in the Fourth Gospel: Narrative Mode and Theological Claim* (Philadelphia: Fortress Press, 1986); Otto Schwankel, "Die Metaphorik von Licht und Finsternis im johanneischen Schrifttum," in Karl Kertelge, ed., *Metaphorik und Mythos im Neuen Testament*, Quaestiones Disputatae 126 (Freiburg: Herder, 1990), 135–67; Thomas Soeding, "Wiedergeburt aus Wasser und Geist: Anmerkungen zur Symbolsprache des Johannesevangeliums am Beispiel des Nikodemusgesprächs (Joh 3, 1–21)," in Kertelge, ed., *Metaphorik und Mythos im Neuen Testament*, 168–219; Robert Kysar, "Johannine Metaphor—Meaning and Function: A Literary Case Study of John 10:1–18," *Semeia* 53, *The Fourth Gospel from a Literary Perspective* (1991) 81–111. Two other studies of Johannine language deserve mention: Franz Mussner, *The Historical Jesus in the Gospel of St. John*, trans. W. J. O'Hara, Quaestiones Disputatae (New York: Herder, 1967), on John's "gnoseological terminology"; and F. M. Braun, "La réduction du Pluriel au Singulier dans l'Évangile et la Premiere Lettre de Jean," *NTS* 24 (1977) 40–67.

  3. See the references in n. 1.

  4. The most influential study is J. Louis Martyn's *History and Theology in the Fourth Gospel* (Nashville: Abingdon, 1968; rev. and enl. 1979). See also his "Source Criticism and *Religionsgeschichte* in the Fourth Gospel," in *Jesus and Man's Hope*, vol. 1 (Pittsburgh: Pittsburgh Theological Seminary, 1970), 247–73, and *The Gospel of John in Christian History: Essays for Interpreters* (New York: Paulist Press, 1978). See further: Oscar Cullmann, *The Johannine Circle*, trans. John Bowden (Philadelphia: Westminster Press, 1976); Raymond E. Brown, *The Community of the Beloved Disciple* (New York: Paulist Press, 1979); D. Moody Smith, *Johannine Christianity: Essays on its Setting, Sources, and Theology* (Columbia, S.C.: University of South Carolina Press, 1984); and Neyrey, *An Ideology of Revolt*.

  5. See the references in n. 4. The focal issue is the specific source of the persecution of Christians represented in John, which Martyn identified with an ancient Jewish anti-Christian prayer. For detailed criticism of this identification, see Reuven Kimelmann, "*Birkat Ha-Minim* and the Lack of Evidence for an Anti-Christian Jewish Prayer in Late Antiquity," in E. P. Sanders et al., eds., *Jewish and Christian Self-Definition*. Vol. 2, *Aspects of Judaism in the Graeco-Roman Period* (Philadelphia: Fortress Press, 1981), 226–44. In this same volume, see the more appreciative assessment of Martyn's thesis by A. F. Segal, "Ruler of This World: Attitudes about Mediator Figures and the Importance of Sociology for Self-Definition," 245–68. See also W. Horbury, "The Benediction of the *Minim* and Early Jewish-Christian Controversy," *JThS* 33 (1982) 19–61.

  6. The topic is as lacking in the commentaries as it is in the several surveys of Johannine scholarship.

  7. I include in the notion of a contrastive style what is usually referred to as Johannine "dualism" or "dualities." See the judicious comments by Duke, *Irony in the Fourth Gospel*, 142–47, which should be read in the context of the entire chapter, "Irony and the Johannine Context," 139–56. Although he concentrates on irony, Duke provides the best discussion of a linguistic phenomenon in its literary and social context. I am less persuaded than he, however, that John's special use of language is comprehensible in the terms of everyday language, a point on which I side, e.g., with Bultmann, Leroy, and Meeks.

  8. As mentioned in n. 1, Leroy and Meeks deserve the credit for seeing that John's special language is the context in which particular linguistic uses must be understood. The present study represents an

attempt to develop both that insight and their insight into its social corollary, which is best expressed in Halliday's notion of an anti-language belonging to an anti-society.

9. Two observations are in order here, the first being that in John's narrative Jesus' disciples do not understand his special use of language any more than the other characters do. The second is that the use of the special language became a community language only after Jesus' departure. Historically, it also means that this language was only created after Jesus' departure and in a social context of believers who were expelled from synagogues and in some cases even executed for being disciples of Jesus. In this light, it is interesting to note that in 1 John, the special language has become the everyday language of its author and his community. Indeed, it is no longer special because the language of 1 John is no longer an anti-language. Corresponding to this difference is the social context of 1 John, which now has to do with in-group problems rather than with persecution by a dominant outside society.

10. The notion of an anti-language legitimating an anti-society's identity, indeed, as being a vehicle of resocialization, originated with Halliday and was picked up from him by Malina (see n. 1). Although Meeks did not know Halliday's work, he nevertheless got the ideas of legitimation and resocialization from the same source as Halliday did, namely Peter L. Berger and Thomas Luckmann's *The Social Construction of Reality: A Treatise in the Sociology of Knowledge* (New York: Doubleday, 1966), the same book that was so important for me in my *Rediscovering Paul: Philemon and the Sociology of Paul's Narrative World* (Philadelphia: Fortress Press, 1985). In that book, I also worked with Victor Turner's notion of structure and anti-structure, and it was in following up on this notion that I first came across Halliday's work. But because my book was by then already in press I could not integrate Halliday's ideas into it. The next time Halliday came up for me was in Malina's essay on John. At the time, I had already embarked on this study and was having too many problems. Malina's use of Halliday helped me to solve them, but it also brought back the categories I had learned from Berger, Luckmann, and Turner. These categories will find their place in this book as well, explicitly in chapters 4 and 5 but implicitly throughout. Finally, mention must be made of Walter Rebell's *Gemeinde als Gegenwelt: Zur soziologischen und didaktischen Funktion des Johannesevangeliums*, BET 20 (Frankfurt: Peter Lang, 1987). Rebell does not know of the work of Halliday and Malina, but he does know of Meek's essay and of Berger and Luckmann. From the latter, he derives the notion of a symbolic universe that legitimates a counter-society. Distinctive of Rebell's argument is his emphasis on the "didactic" function of John's symbolic universe and of his narrative. Unlike Leroy, Malina, and Meeks, however,

Rebell is concerned with John's symbolic universe, not with his special language.

Chapter 1. The Narrator's Use of Language in John 1:1–18

1. In this and the following sentence, certain terms are used in their technical sense in linguistic semantics: 'mean', 'sense', 'denote', and 'refer'. Because the terms are used differently by students of language, I will follow the definitions of John Lyons in his classic *Semantics*, 2 vols. (Cambridge: Cambridge University Press, 1977), 1:1–5 (on meaning), and 1:174–229 (on "Reference, Sense, and Denotation"). Lyons discusses the various uses of the terms, establishes definitions, and provides examples. Like Lyons, I will use the words 'mean' and 'meaning' rather loosely to refer to their linguistic 'sense' and their extralinguistic 'denotation'. 'Sense' is a relationship that obtains "between the words or expressions of a single language independently of the relationship, if any, which holds between those words or expressions and their referents or denotata" (1, 206). 'Sense' is what appears in dictionary entries on words, although these entries also often include denotations. 'Denotation' differs from 'sense' because to 'denote' something is to point to classes of "persons, places, properties, processes and activities external to the language-system" (1, 207). For example, the word 'cow' has a sense that is different from that of the word 'horse', while both words denote classes of animals (cf. 1, 210). 'Reference', however, is not a property of words, but a function of their use in individual utterances or expressions to 'refer' to things, be they concrete, abstract, or fictional (cf. 1, 183). Individual words and expressions have both sense and denotation, but only expressions have reference insofar as they identify "whatever we are talking about when we make a statement about something" (1, 23). For a much briefer account of semantic issues, see F. R. Palmer, *Semantics*, 2d ed. (Cambridge: Cambridge University Press, 1981), 1–43. Two other works pertinent to our concerns are Roger Fowler, *Linguistic Criticism* (Oxford: Oxford University Press, 1986), and Janet Martin Soskice, *Metaphor and Religious Language* (Oxford: Clarendon Press, 1985; pbk. 1988).

2. Walter Bauer, W. F. Arndt, F. W. Gingrich, and F. W. Danker, *A Greek-English Lexicon of the New Testament and Other Early Christian Literature*, 2d ed. (Chicago: University of Chicago Press, 1979), 203–4. John uses both meanings, but in 1:14 the word denotes 'luminosity', as it does in 12:41 (cf. Bultmann, *The Gospel of John*, 67–68, n. 2). In 12:43, however, the word denotes 'honor' or 'praise'. Clearly, John here plays with the two meanings of the word, and he is probably doing the same thing in 5:1–44; 7:18; and 8:49–54 (cf. 17:5, 24).

3. See the brief comments in the introduction (and in n. 1 to that

chapter), and for further discussion see Chapter 4. On John's use of everyday language, we must remember that he has created the speeches of the characters who use it. But in addition to this, many of the so-called asides by the narrator also reflect his use of it. See, e.g., John J. O'Rourke, "Asides in the Gospel of John," *NovT* 21 (1979) 210–19.

4. Bauer et al., *A Greek-English Lexicon of the New Testament*, 477–79. As Bauer shows, the Greek word *logos* ('word') has the sense of 'an act of speech', although it also has the sense of 'reason' or 'motive'. On the other hand, depending on the context of usage, it can denote different classes of speech, such as 'statement', 'question', 'report', etc. In John, however, it is used with the definite article to denote the personification of the 'Word', and because this "Word became flesh" it is mythologized. For this reason, critics have sought the mythological meaning of the word, and many have located this meaning in a strand of ancient Judaism in which the 'Word' of God and the 'Wisdom' (Sophia) of God are synonymous representations of the personified or mythologized 'Wisdom'/'Word' of God. In addition to the commentaries, see further, e.g., James D. G. Dunn, *Christology in the Making: A New Testament Inquiry into the Origins of the Doctrine of the Incarnation* (Philadelphia: Westminster, 1980), 213–50, and Dunn, "Let John Be John: A Gospel for Its Time," in Peter Stuhlmacher, ed., *The Gospel and the Gospels* (Grand Rapids: Eerdmans, 1991), 293–322, esp. 314–20. On the 'Wisdom' (Sophia) of God, see Chapter 5. For an extended discussion of research on the prologue, see Michael Theobald, *Die Fleischwerdung des Logos: Studien zum Verhältnis des Johannesprologs zum Corpus des Evangeliums und zu 1 John*, NTAbh 20 (Münster: Aschendorff, 1988).

5. In the Greek text of 1:1c, the clause has the word 'God' appear first, without a definite article: "and God was the Word." Critics agree that the lack of the definite article here, and its presence before "the Word," renders 'God' as the predicate of the statement, "the Word was God." Critics disagree, however, over whether or not the word 'God' has the adjectival sense and denotation of 'divine'. The principal recent proponent of this view is Ernst Haenchen, *John [Vol.] 1: A Commentary of the Gospel of John, Chapters 1–6*, trans. R. W. Funk, Hermeneia (Philadelphia: Fortress Press, 1984), 109–11. I agree with Bultmann's arguments against this interpretation and with his recognition that what is at issue is the "equality" of the 'Word' with 'God' (*The Gospel of John*, 33–35). Bultmann also rightly observes that the statement in 1:1c contradicts the statement in 1:1b, and he is perhaps correct in terming the contradiction a paradox. On the other hand, however, from the perspective of John's use of language, the contradictions that we will observe throughout the prologue raise more fundamental semantic issues.

The notion that 'God' is the predicate of the clause raises a further semantic issue, for while it is a grammatical predicate, the verb "was" is an equative rather than a predicative copula. Here we must again refer to Lyons, who makes two important distinctions. The first is that between referring expressions, which identify *what* we are talking about, and predicative expressions, which "ascribe particular properties to whatever is being referred to." Thus, "we can use 'Boston' to refer to Boston and we can predicate of Boston the expression 'populous' in order to ascribe it to the property of being populous" (1, 23). The second distinction, which pertains to the meaning of 1:1c, is between the predicative and equative uses of the copula 'to be'. In an equative sentence containing two referring expressions, the two expressions are interchangeable, whereas in a predicative sentence the two noun phrases are not interchangeable; one phrase is a referring expression and the other is a predicative expression. In his example of two readings of the sentence, "Giscard d'Estaing is the President of France," Lyons explains that in addition to the possibility that "the President of France" is a predicative expression, it could also be a referring expression in which "the copula asserts an identity between two referents" (1, 185). In Lyons's terms, the statement in 1:1c contains two referring expressions and an equative copula which asserts the identity of their referents. John therefore renders the words 'God' and the 'Word' synonymous, and we will find that the semantic synonymy created by the use of words having different senses and denotations to refer to one referent is a distinctive feature of John's special language.

6. See n. 5, above, on the synonymy created by the equative copula in 1:1c. Synonymy in everyday language is a matter of "sameness of meaning" (Palmer, *Semantics*, 88; cf. 88–93), or of "'having the same sense', not [of] 'having the same reference'" (Lyons, *Semantics 1*, 199). In John's special use of language, however, words having *different* senses and denotations in everyday language are rendered synonymous when he uses them to refer to the same thing. John *creates* synonyms and, according to Halliday, this is a characteristic of anti-languages, which are typically overlexicalized as a result of their density of synonyms for the same thing (*Language as Social Semiotic*, 167–68). John is different from the samples cited by Halliday, because John uses common words to refer to uncommon things; but this is in itself an anti-language phenomenon, because John's use is opposed to everyday use.

7. For a brief discussion that uses terms somewhat differently from Lyons, yet is to the point, see Oswald Ducrot and Tzvetan Todorov, *Encyclopedic Dictionary of the Sciences of Language*, trans. C. Porter (Baltimore: Johns Hopkins University Press, 1979), 101–2. For a fuller

and much more technical discussion, see Umberto Eco, *Semiotics and the Philosophy of Language* (Bloomington: Indiana University Press, 1984), 130–63.

8. Soskice, *Metaphor and Religious Language*, 15. The literature on metaphor is enormous, but Soskice provides a sound critical review and an extensive bibliography. For a more technical discussion see, again, Eco, *Semiotics and the Philosophy of Language*, 87–129.

9. See n. 5, above, and Soskice, *Metaphor and Religious Language*, 54–66, on metaphor and simile.

10. See n. 5, above.

11. The Greek word *katalambanein* has both meanings, and John may well be playing on this, as C. K. Barrett notes in *The Gospel According to John: An Introduction with Commentary and Notes on the Greek Text*, 2d ed. (Philadelphia: Westminster Press, 1978), 158–59. However, the parallelism between *ou katelaben* and *ouk egno* and *ou parelabon* in vv. 10–11 suggest that John uses the three verbs synonymously to mean 'receive' or 'understand'. Cf. Bultmann, *The Gospel of John*, 48 n. 1, and below on further synonyms in the prologue. Other critics find that 'overcome' better fits the relationship between light and darkness. Cf. Raymond E. Brown, *The Gospel According to John, 1–12: Introduction, Translation, and Notes*, Anchor (Garden City, N.Y.: Doubleday, 1966), 8.

12. See most recently Schwankel, "Die Metaphorik von Licht und Finsternis im johanneischen Schrifttum." I agree with Bultmann, *The Gospel of John*, 40, that in this instance 'light' is not spoken of figuratively; see further 40–45 on the varieties of usage in John, and for further discussion of the problems of distinguishing between figurative and literal usage, Hans Conzelmann, "Phos, ktl," in Gerhard Friedrich, ed., *Theological Dictionary of the New Testament*, vol. 9, trans. G. W. Bromiley (Grand Rapids: Eerdmans, 1974), 349–53.

13. In the expression "true light" in v. 9, "true" stands in contrast with the statements in vv. 6–8 concerning John the Baptist, who is said to have been a "witness to the light," but "not the light." His "light" was only that of "a burning and shining lamp" (5:35).

14. Precisely because of the relationship between vv. 5 and 9, commentators differ on which meaning is intended.

15. See n. 2, above, and for discussion of the 'glory' of Israel's God, Chapter 4.

16. See the commentaries for discussions of the issues and compare translations for the variety of readings that have been proposed.

17. In the other two instances of *monogenes* in John, this word is accompanied by "the Son": *ton huion ton monogene*, 3:16; *tou monogenous huiou tou theou*, 3:18. These together with the references to "the Father" in 1:14 and 18, require us to read *monogenes* as a reference to the Father's

"only Son." On the word *monogenes*, see the commentaries. For further discussion of the significance of the word in John, see Chapter 5.

18. Critics agree that 1:14–18 is a distinct section within the prologue, and most note the narrator's claim to be among those who had an experience of the Word's glory. Discussion tends, however, to focus on source-critical matters, history-of-religions backgrounds, historical reliability, and theological issues. My pointing to the narrator's shift in point of view is in the interest of both literary and sociological concerns, for here he identifies himself with a group of people who are socially opposed to and by others who did not "receive" what had come into the world (1:9–13). These matters are discussed further in the present chapter and in Chapter 4. Some of the history of religions and source questions, on the other hand, are addressed in Chapter 5.

19. Although Dunn, in "Let John be John" (317–20), speaks out of history of religions and theological concerns, he rightly sees that John's Father/Son language must be read in light of the role of the Word. Indeed, he observes that "while 'Son' is more fitted to express distinction and relation . . . , 'Logos' [Word] by definition better expresses sameness and continuity" (318). See further Bultmann, *The Gospel of John*, 248–54.

20. Other systems are discussed in Chapter 3.

21. See further Chapter 3.

22. See, e.g., Bultmann, *The Gospel of John*, 54–56, and Mussner, *The Historical Jesus in the Gospel of St. John*, 17–47.

23. Cf. 14:17, and Bultmann, *The Gospel of John*, 76 n. 5.

24. Bultmann, *The Gospel of John*, 73–74, describes "grace and truth" as a "hendiadys," which means saying one thing by means of two words, and he notes that these words "describe God's being; not 'in itself', but . . . [as] the benefits in which God (or the Revealer) abounds, and which he bestows on the believer." He also observes that in John "truth" has "the meaning of 'divine reality', with the connotation that this reality *reveals* itself" (74 n. 2). See also Bultmann, *Theology of the New Testament* 2, 18–19: "Truth is not the teaching about God transmitted by Jesus but is God's very reality revealing itself—occurring!—in Jesus" (19). Bultmann does not speak of the synonymy of 'grace' and 'truth' with 'God', 'the Word', and 'the Light', but because the latter three terms also connote self-disclosure as well as 'being', and because all five terms refer to the same entity, they are synonymous with one another.

25. See, e.g., Bultmann, *Theology of the New Testament* 2, 15–17.

26. In discussing 1:5 and 1:9 earlier, I said that v. 9 is a metaphor for v. 5, and I cited the anthropomorphic metaphors in v. 9. However, I did not cite "the world" as a metaphor because it is clear that for John

it is synonymous with "darkness." The semantic relationship between these two words is quite different, e.g., from the relationship between "shines" and "comes into," in which the latter is a metaphor for the former.

27. Like "Father" and "Son," "sons of Light" and "children of God" are metaphors denoting separation and difference, while in both cases John envisions an ultimate unity, although he does not elaborate this beyond what we see in 17:11–26.

28. If Bultmann's views of John are stripped on the one hand of his history-of-religions emphasis on a gnostic revealer myth, and on the other hand of his existentialist theological interpretation of "faith," he comes very close to making the same observations I have made about the Other and its reception. For example, consider several statements made in his *Theology of the New Testament* 2: John "presents only the fact (*dass Dass*) of the Revelation without describing its content (*ihr Was*)" (66); his "Jesus brought no 'doctrine' capable of being summarized in propositions; his word . . . is he himself" (90); "Jesus' words communicate no definable content at all, except that they are words of life, words of God, not because of their content, but because of whose words they are" (63); Jesus "*reveals nothing but that he is the Revealer*" (66). And faith is not a volitional act, but only an effect of "God's working on" the believer (23). Although I find Bultmann's notion of "the decision of faith" overly intentional on the believer's part (see further 70–88), it is nevertheless clear that for John 'faith' means something quite different from what it means in everyday language (i.e., "I believe that . . ."), and this is evident in the synonymy of a number of expressions: "Certain figurative expressions mean the same thing" (70), and "Jesus and his words are identical"; and his "works . . . are identical with his words" (71; cf. 63). For further discussion of some of these issues, and for a critique of Bultmann from a literary and theological perspective, see O'Day, *Revelation in the Fourth Gospel*. O'Day, however, only confronts the linguistic problems in terms of irony, and she believes that John's language *is* comprehensible when properly decoded.

29. See Chapter 3.

30. For discussions of opposition and contrast, see Lyons, *Semantics* 1, 270–90, and Palmer, *Semantics*, 94–100.

31. As Bultmann notes, this reference is expressed in the metaphorical language of a spatial relationship, but this is masked by the temporal sense of the English words "after" and "before" (*The Gospel of John*, 75).

32. See Martyn, *History and Theology in the Fourth Gospel*, 130–43, and more fully, Wayne A. Meeks, *The Prophet-King: Moses Traditions and the Johannine Christology*, SNovT, 14 (Leiden: Brill, 1967), 297–301, and

"The Man from Heaven in Johannine Sectarianism." Meeks locates the "seeing" of God in the context of traditions dealing with both ascent and descent and descent and ascent. See further Chapter 4.

33. I speak of 'contrasts' in Lyons' sense, as noted in n. 30, above. See also Duke, *Irony in the Fourth Gospel*, 142–47, who prefers 'duality' over the more frequently used notion of 'dualism'.

34. See further Chapter 4, and the bibliographical discussion in n. 1 to the Introduction to this volume.

Chapter 2. Language and Characterization 1: How Jesus Speaks

1. See Chapter 4 on the forensic character of the questions asked by the "priests and Levites" who had been sent from Jerusalem by "the Jews." For the moment, it will suffice to note that the Baptist's response is identified as a 'confession' (1:20), which is consistent with the narrator's references to him giving 'testimony' and 'bearing witness' (1:7, 15, 19, 32). Cf. Bultmann, *The Gospel of John*, 50 n. 5, and 82–83.

2. On naming as a means of characterization, see Bultmann, *The Gospel of John*, 72 n. 2, and for a broader literary discussion of this, see Boris Uspensky, *A Poetics of Composition: The Structure of the Artistic Text and a Typology of Compositional Form*, trans. Valentina Zavarin and S. Wittig (Berkeley: University of California Press, 1973), 20–31, 121–22, 161–62.

3. "The Messiah" is in the form of a Greek transliteration of the Aramaic.

4. Bultmann notes that while the word "Rabbi" is used by the disciples and others as a gesture of respect, this "form of address brings out the paradox that the Son of God appears as a Jewish Rabbi" (*The Gospel of John*, 100 n. 5; cf. 1:49; 3:2; 4:31; 6:25; 11:8, 28; 20:16; cf. 13:13). For ironic aspects of the notion of Jesus as a Rabbi, see Duke, *Irony in the Fourth Gospel*, 71–73.

5. On the distinction between the adjective 'true' and the adverb 'truly', see Meeks, "The Man from Heaven in Johannine Sectarianism," 52 n. 28.

6. The alternative to the Word becoming incarnate in an already existing human being would be for the Word to have been 'born' as Jesus. But as Bultmann observes, being 'born' "is oriented to the viewpoint of Pilate," who sees the man Jesus, while "the origin . . . of this man is not from this world, but he has 'come' into this world" (*The Gospel of John*, 655). Like the process by which believers become children of God, the Word's becoming flesh as the only Son from the Father is a birth "not of blood nor of the will of the flesh nor of the will of man, but of God" (1:13). Although John does not spell out his understanding of

either process, he would appear to be closer to the notion of Athena taking on the human forms of already existing males, Mentes and Mentor (*Odyssey*, Books 1–4), or to Raphael becoming Azarias (Tobit), than to the kind of birth represented in the birth stories of Matthew and Luke.

7. For example, 6:42. The issue is more fully discussed in Chapter 4.

8. The subordination of Moses is also implied in 1:18 and 5:37, both of which are also discussed in Chapter 4, where we will address John's use of the image of Moses in his characterization of Jesus.

9. See the references in Chap. 1, n. 32, and Chapter 4.

10. Bultmann, *The Gospel of John*, 105 n. 3, attributes the identification of Jesus with Jacob's ladder to Odeberg and Strack, but he himself thinks John has in mind "the uninterrupted communion between Jesus and the Father." The disciples will see the Father in him (ibid., 106). Barrett, *The Gospel According to St. John*, 186–87, discusses other options and dismisses the idea that the Word is the ladder. Like Bultmann, he sees the Son of Man as "an eternal contact between heaven and earth," and the ladder as an expression of this concept (187). For a fuller review of pertinent history of religions material, see Hugo Odeberg, *The Fourth Gospel: Interpreted in Its Relation to Contemporaneous Religious Currents in Palestine and the Hellenistic-Oriental World* (1929; Chicago: Argonaut, 1968), 33–42.

11. The several synonymous systems are considered in Chapter 3.

12. See Bultmann, *Theology of the New Testament* 2, 44–47, and esp. 59–61, where he discusses *"the identity of work and word"* (61).

13. Cf. Duke, *Irony in the Fourth Gospel*, 83–84 and 95–97, on ironic characterization and the irony of identity.

14. As noted earlier, the role of the image of Moses in John's system of characterization and in the plot of his story is fully discussed in Chapter 4.

15. In one version ("E"), the sign is for Moses himself (3:12), while in the other ("J") signs are for those to whom Moses has been sent (4:1–9). In the former, the sign is the coming to pass of an event announced in advance by God; in the latter, the signs are magical: a rod that turns into a snake and back; a hand that turns leprous and then returns to normal; and water that turns into blood. While the latter are closed related to Jesus' "signs" in John, the former is also found in John in conjunction with the distinction between a true or false prophet like Moses, based on Deut. 18:22. See Meeks, *The Prophet-King*, 45–46, and Chapter 4.

16. See Bultmann, *Theology of the New Testament* 2: *"the works of Jesus . . . are his words"* (60); *"his word is identical with himself"* (63). See

also his *The Gospel of John*, 227: "Jesus *gives* the bread of life in that he *is* the bread of life."

17. Cf. Bultmann, *Theology of the New Testament* 2: "As 'signs' the miracles of Jesus are ambiguous. Like Jesus' words, they are misunderstandable" (44). "What is true of the miracles is true of all that Jesus does: it is not understood" (45).

18. Cf. ibid., 44: Jesus' signs (and words) "are remarkable occurrences, but that only makes them indicators that the activity of the Revealer is a disturbance of what is familiar to the world." And from *The Gospel of John*: "The ambiguity of Johannine concepts and statements which lead to misunderstandings does not consist in one word having two meanings, so that the misunderstanding comes as a result of choosing the wrong one; it is rather that there are concepts and statements, which at first sight refer to earthly matters, but properly refer to divine matters. The misunderstanding comes when someone sees the right meaning of the word but mistakenly imagines that its meaning is exhausted by the reference to earthly matters" (135 n. 1).

19. Because John understands the "temple" to be Jesus' body (2:21), the reference to it taking forty-six years to build the temple may be an allusion to Jesus' age; cf. 8:57 and the comment that Jesus was "not yet fifty years old." See, e.g., Barrett, *The Gospel According to St. John*, 352; Brown, *The Gospel According to John* 1, 116, and Bultmann, *The Gospel of John*, 127 n. 3.

20. No mention is made of how Jesus' audience understood his reference to "my Father," but in light of the prologue the narrator is here nudging *his* audience, which knows what the characters in the story do not know.

21. There is some confusion in the sequence of actions here, for the crowd hails Jesus' entry into Jerusalem before Jesus finds the young ass upon which he enters the city. Because the narrator makes his comment immediately after the reference to Jesus' finding the ass, and the accompanying scriptural quotation, it is likely that he relocated the former from its original position in his source—in order to make his own point about the disciples' ignorance.

22. These synonyms and others are discussed further in the next section on 3:1–15, 31–36.

23. See Chap. 1, n. 28.

24. The coming of the Holy Spirit referred to here is probably not the in-breathing of the Holy Spirit mentioned in 20:22, which is rather related to matters of church discipline (20:23).

25. 3:16–21 is a continuation of Jesus' speech in vv. 10–15, but it is in the narrator's special language, as are vv. 31–36, which are a continuation of the Baptist's speech in vv. 27–30. Both vv. 16–21 and 31–36 are

probably to be understood as the narrator's speech to his audience. Vv. 16–21 will be discussed in different contexts in each of the next three chapters. Here we are concerned with how Jesus speaks.

26. See n. 18, above, for a quotation from Bultmann on multiple meanings and the problem of reference.

27. See Barrett, *The Gospel According to St. John:* "The Spirit, like the wind, is entirely beyond the control and the comprehension of man: It breathes into this world from another" (211). See also Brown, *The Gospel According to John,* 1, 141, and Bultmann, *The Gospel of John,* 142.

28. See the references to Meeks in Chap. 1, n. 32, and chapters 4 and 5.

29. On the face of it, v. 13 could be understood to be referring to the Son of Man's having ascended into heaven and then descending in order to do what he was sent to do. For Peder Borgen, "Some Jewish Exegetical Traditions as Background for Son of Man Sayings in John's Gospel (Jn 3, 1314 and context)" (in M. De Jonge, ed., *L'Évangile de Jean: Sources, redaction, theologie,* BETL 44 [Leuven: Duculot, 1977], 243–58), 3:13–14 refers to an ascent into heaven for his installation into office, a descent to execute his charge, and to a return to the position of his pre-existent enthronement. A similar conclusion has been drawn independently of Borgen by Jan-A. Bühner in *Der Gesandte und sein Weg im 4. Evangelium: Die kultur und religionsgeschichtlichen Grundlagen der johanneischen Sendungschristologie sowie ihre traditionsgeschichtliche Entwicklung,* WANT 2 (Tübingen: Mohr, 1977). For a critique of their arguments, see Francis J. Moloney, *The Johannine Son of Man,* 2d ed., Biblioteca di Scienze Religiose, 14 (Rome: LAS, 1978), 230–44. On the other hand, Moloney reads 3:13–14 quite differently from most commentators because he sees no reference to the Son of Man's ascent in 3:13–14 or 6:62 or, indeed, in John at all. He only allows for the descent of the Son of Man. For a critique of Moloney's argument, see Godfrey C. Nicholson, *Death as Departure: The Johannine Descent-Ascent Schema,* SBLDS, 63 (Chico: Scholars Press, 1983), especially 93–95. The weakness of Moloney's argument is that it is oriented only to what is said of the Son of Man, whereas Nicholson recognizes a fundamental descent/ascent schema which underlies several different designations of Jesus and several different terminological systems for representing his coming and going. We will develop this insight in Chapter 3, in addition to some observations in this chapter about the synonymy of a number of terms that are used to describe Jesus' return whence he came.

30. Nicholson deals with the lifting-up sayings in the context of the descent/ascent schema. For exegetical discussions of the relevant passages, see *Death as Departure,* 75–160.

31. The everyday language of v. 32 is indicated in v. 33, where the narrator explains that Jesus "said this to show by what death he was to die." However, this everyday understanding is also understood by the reader in special language terms. As Nicholson has shown, Jesus' death is part of the process of his return whence he came (*Death as Departure,* 124–51).

32. Although he does not speak of synonymy, Nicholson rightly sees that these terms represent Jesus' return (cf. *Death as Departure,* 141–51).

33. This was Wrede's basic thesis for all of the Gospels in his *Messianic Secret.* Although he saw the post-resurrection new understanding(s) as reflecting a historical fact, he drew this conclusion as an inference from his literary analysis and used it to explain the literary phenomena.

34. See above on 1:43–51.

35. Viewing 10:7b and 9 as interpolations makes better sense of what Jesus says, although it is not beyond possibility that they are part of a special language play, adding to the notion that Jesus is "the Lamb of God" (1:29, 36) the notions that he is also "the door of the sheep" and "the good shepherd." If these verses are not interpolations, they would contribute to a quintessential example of referent blurring. Bultmann, *The Gospel of John,* 359, suggests that vv. 7 and 9 "are the Evangelist's glosses" on his source, but Barrett, for example, sees no need for such a suggestion and rather sees the verses as representing a magnification of the figure of Jesus by applying "every epithet which the picture of sheep and shepherd suggests" (*The Gospel According to St. John,* 370–73).

36. See Bultmann, *The Gospel of John,* 63: "But this is the paradox which runs through the whole gospel: the *doxa* [glory] is not to be seen *alongside* the *sarx* [flesh] nor *through* the *sarx* as through a window; it is to be seen in the *sarx* and nowhere else. If man wishes to see the *doxa,* then it is on the *sarx* that he must concentrate his attention, without allowing himself to fall a victim to appearances. The revelation is present in a peculiar *hiddenness*" (cf. 69, where the flesh is the object of seeing, but of a seeing that "is neither sensory nor spiritual, but it is the sight of *faith*").

Chapter 3. Language and Characterization 1:
What Jesus Speaks About

1. See Chap. 2, n. 19.

2. See Chap. 2, n. 6.

3. For a typologies of "I am" sayings, see Bultmann, *The Gospel of John,* 225 n. 3 (also, *Theology of the New Testament* 2, 64–66), and Brown,

The Gospel According to John, 1, 533–38. See the commentaries for discussion of individual passages. For more detailed discussion of predicateless "I am" sayings, see Philip B. Harner, *The "I Am" of the Fourth Gospel*, Facet Books, BibSer, 26 (Philadelphia: Fortress Press, 1970).

4. 10:36 is not in the same form as the other "I am X" statements because it lacks the first person singular personal pronoun "I" (*ego*) and because the verb appears after the predicate. It is also the case that here Jesus is quoting himself, although his original statement is not narrated. Nevertheless, it is a first-person self-identification. We should probably interpret 4:26, where Jesus says in another variant of the "I am X" form that he is the Messiah, in the light of 10:36 and of the several synonymous royal identifications in 1:29–51, among which are Son of God and Messiah. In 4:26, moreover, it is the Samaritan woman who introduces the notion of Messiah (4:25), not Jesus, who only says, "I who speak to you am he." For a third-person self-identification as Son of Man, see 9:35–37.

5. See Chap. 1, n. 24, and for a dissenting view, Ignace de la Potterie, "The Truth in Saint John," in John Ashton, ed., *The Interpretation of John*, Issues in Religion and Theology, 9 (Philadelphia: Fortress Press, 1986), 53–66 (the article originally appeared in 1963). De la Potterie's case is weakened when in explaining "I am the truth" he finds it necessary "to contemplate the mystery of his [Jesus'] person, the mystery of the trinitarian relationship between Father and Son" (58). I rather think that the mystery is located in John's mystifying use of language.

6. On 'Light', see 1:9, 3:19, 8:12, 9:5 (cf. 9:39), 12:35–36, 46; 'prophet', 6:14, cf. 7:40–42, 52; 'Messiah/Christ', 4:25 (cf. 4:42), and 11:27, where 'Christ' is synonymous with 'the Son of God'. See also 7:26–28, 31, 41–42, and probably 18:37, where Jesus' reference to his coming into the world is related to his being 'King of the Jews', which in 1:49 is synonymous with the 'Son of God', on which see 11:27. The only anomaly is in 16:28, where 'coming into the world' is predicated of 'the Son of the Father', but that is in John's special language, whereas 'the Messiah/Christ' predications are in everyday language.

7. As we will see shortly, Jesus' glorification is related to the Word system because "he" is returning to the glory which "he," as the Word, had "before the world was made" (cf. 17:5, 24).

8. 'Darkness' implicitly completes the Light system because when the Light ceases to be in the world darkness implicitly reigns. Cf. 8:12, 9:4–5, 11:9–10, and 12:35–36.

9. Cf. 12:34.

10. In Mark, the Son of Man only comes from heaven in the narrator's eschatological future (cf. 8:38–9:1, 13:24–27).

11. In the Wisdom of Solomon, all righteous persons are God's sons and they boast that God is their Father (2:16–18).

12. In Chapter 5 we will consider the relationship between the Father/Son system and the Word system in light of a system associated with the personified Wisdom (Sophia) of God. As for this Wisdom system, although the Wisdom texts represent different systems, John either knows of a single one containing elements of the different ones or he creates a single one out of those he knows.

13. See the discussion of John 3 in Chapter 2.

14. In 12:41 Isaiah's vision of the glory of God in Isaiah 6 is said to have been a vision of Jesus' glory, but this must be understood as the preincarnate glory of the Word (cf. 1:14). Note also the play on the meanings of *doxa* as 'honor'/'glory' in 12:43, where the second occurrence of the word bears the meaning 'glory of God'. Note, too, the references to Jesus as the Light in 12:35–36, 46, and the juxtaposition of glorification and being 'lifted up' in 12:28–34. In 12:20–50 we find the Father/Son system, the Light system, and the Son of Man system, and in 12:23 it is said that the Son of Man's hour of glorification has come, which appears to be synonymous with his being 'lifted up' in 12:31–34. For further discussion see Moloney, *The Johannine Son of Man*, 176–85, where, however, he limits himself to the Son of Man material (except for 208–14) and Nicholson, *Death as Departure*, 141–50, for a more balanced treatment.

15. On the Son of Man in John, see Moloney, *The Johannine Son of Man*, which despite its previously noted limitations is nevertheless a useful study of the texts and critical debate. As noted, too, Nicholson, *Death as Departure*, has a better sense of the descent/ascent structure that underlies John's overall characterization of Jesus.

16. See Moloney, *The Johannine Son of Man*, 87–123, but again with a focus on the Son of Man.

17. In 6:25 there is in addition to the synonymy of 'coming to me' and 'believing in me' also a synonymy between 'not hungering' and 'never thirsting'. In John 6, 'not hungering' is contrasted with the death of the fathers who ate the mannah in the wilderness, yet died (6:48–51b). For a parallel contrast associated with 'never thirsting', see 4:13–14. These contrasts are discussed further in Chapter 4.

18. Despite the Son of Man identifier (6:27) and the related notion of his descent, the several references in 6:25–65 to the 'Father', and especially to having been 'sent' by the Father, are derived from the Father/Son system, as is the notion of 'eternal life'. The presence of this system is guaranteed by the relationship between 6:46 and 1:18. On the Son of Man as judge, see Moloney, *The Johannine Son of Man*, 68–86.

19. Although he notes the frequent references to Moses, Moloney fails to see the persistent play on the relationship between Jesus and Moses, a play that is not limited to the Son of Man system, as we will see in Chapter 4.

20. They are also present in John's narrative because it, too, makes belief possible (17:20, 19:35, 29:29–31).

21. See Bultmann, *Theology of the New Testament* 2, 33–69.

22. Although Odeberg's comments are overly oriented to "mystical meaning," he suggestively observes the analogy between light being in one and such other Johannine locutions as "truth in him" (8:44), having "the love of God within you" (5:42–43), and "my word abiding in you" (5:38; cf. 8:37, 15:4–5; *The Fourth Gospel*, 333). But these locutions seem to belong to John's anthropology, which is represented in other related locutions, such as the Father and the Son having life in themselves (5:26; cf. 1:4), the Father being in the Son and the Son in the Father, and the Son being in believers and he in them (10:38; 14:10–11, 20; 17:21–23). Also, the notions of 'having' a demon (8:48–49, 52; 10:20–21) [cf. Satan *entering* Judas, 13:27], 'having' 'Light of Life' (8:12); and 'having' 'Light' (12:36) should be added to Odeberg's analogies. What is suggestive about the statements involving the presence of something positive being in one is that there is a relationship of synonymy between the terms describing the positive something, e.g., Life, Light, Truth, love of God, Jesus' words, the Son, and the Father.

23. The correspondence is self-evident, but we cannot know whether or not speculation on the experience of looking into the sun led John to the idea of nondifferentiation and its linguistic representation in referent blurring. While Bultmann does not see John as a mystic, he does see that "the mystic gaze beholds the divine light, in which all duality disappears, and nothing more that is individual can be recognized, and in which consciousness of the self finally fades away . . . [W]hat is dominant here is the longing for definitive self-understanding, which the duality, the separation of subject and object, is felt to destroy" (*The Gospel of John*, 43 n. 2).

24. See Duke, *Irony in the Fourth Gospel*, 142–47.

Chapter 4. The Sociology of Light

1. The distinction between situation and response is different from the distinction between social systems and symbolic systems, or social institutions and symbolic universes, that I dealt with in *Rediscovering Paul*. Although the response *is* symbolic and as such legitimates the Johannine community, it is more the existence of the community that is legitimated than its institutions. But our concern is rather with the relationship between the content of the symbolic response and the

community's social situation and, indeed, the symbolic universe of the institutions to which the community is opposed. The immediate precursor to this approach is Meeks, "The Man from Heaven in Johannine Sectarianism."

2. The qualification "as John represents it" is intended to emphasize the literary rather than historical focus of this study. It is his representation of a social situation that is of concern, not the accuracy of what he says or the particular historical circumstances of that situation. For discussion of the latter, see, e.g., the references cited in nn. 4 and 5 to the Introduction.

3. In view of the disclaimer in the previous note, I should like to add to the references referred to there two studies of the Apocalypse of John that take up the notion of deprivation as a socially causal phenomenon: Adela Yarbro Collins, "Revelation 18: Taunt-Song or Dirge?," in J. Lambrecht, ed., *L'Apocalypse johannique et l'apocalyptique dans le Nouveau Testament* (Gembloux: Duculot, 1980), 185–204, and Leonard Thompson, "A Sociological Analysis of Tribulation in the Apocalypse of John," *Semeia* 36 (1986) 147–74. Their point, and that of relative deprivation theorists, is that the critical factor is the perception of deprivation, or in the Gospel's case, of rejection, not the actual degree of historical deprivation or rejection. In other words, to look for some extratextual occasion that might be proportionate to the deprivation represented in the text could be misleading. In this light, what I am describing is John's perception and representation of the situation, although for reasons of style this qualification is not made beyond the opening remarks of the chapter.

4. See n. 1 to the Introduction for discussion and literature.

5. See especially Meeks, "The Man from Heaven in Johannine Sectarianism."

6. This is a large part of Burton L. Mack's theory about the Gospel of Mark, *A Myth of Innocence: Mark and Christian Origins* (Philadelphia: Fortress Press, 1988). I find the theory more appropriate to John than to Mark. My critique of Mack's book was made in an unpublished paper presented to the Literary Aspects Group of the SBL in 1989, "Literary Criticism, Social History, and the Gospel According to Mark." While not engaging Mack's book, the literary evidence for a view counter to his may be found in my "'Literarkritik', the New Literary Criticism, and the Gospel According to Mark," in *The Four Gospels 1992*, Festschrift Franz Neirynck, BETL C, ed. F. Van Segbroeck et al. (Leuven: University Press, 1992), 935–48.

7. See especially Martyn, *History and Theology in the Fourth Gospel*, 24–62. Martyn used John 9 to introduce his argument that John's episodes operate on two levels, one having to do with Jesus' time and the

other with his own. But Bultmann, *The Gospel of John*, 239, had already argued that John 5 and 9 reflect issues in John's time.

8. See Martyn, *History and Theology in the Fourth Gospel*, 64–89, and Meeks, *The Prophet-King*, 47–57, on the Deuteronomic notion of the 'false prophet' who leads astray.

9. The characterization of the Pharisee Nicodemus also seems to reflect fear of the authorities, since he first went to see Jesus at night, rather than publicly (3:2), then risks a legal defense of Jesus (7:50–52), and then joins Joseph of Arimathea, who was a disciple of Jesus who "for fear of the Jews" secretly went to Pilate to request that Jesus' body be turned over to him for burial (19:38–42). Because the narrator explicitly refers to the fact that Nicodemus had first gone to Jesus at night (19:39) in the context of Joseph's fearful secret maneuver, the nighttime visit may have been motivated by the same fear. See Jouette M. Bassler, "Mixed Signals: Nicodemus in the Fourth Gospel," *JBL* 108 (1989) 635–46. Note, too, that Judas' betrayal took place at night (18:3).

10. As we will see in the next section, the inversion of terms is an anti-structural operation. See Victor Turner, *The Ritual Process: Structure and Anti-Structure* (Chicago: Aldine Press, 1969), and for a broader view of inversion, Barbara A. Babcock, ed., *The Reversible World: Symbolic Inversion in Art and Society* (Ithaca: Cornell *University Press*, 1978). Neyrey, *An Ideology of Revolt*, 115–50, uses Mary Douglas's grid/group theory to trace the history of the Johannine community and sees the anti-stance as being the last of three stages. His concern, however, is with the Christology developed in this stage.

11. For other approaches to such stages, see the literature cited in n. 4 to the Introduction. Although there are both similarities and differences between my staging and those of others, my argument is intended to lay out the inversion of polarized points of view as a basis for discussing John's special language as the anti-language of an anti-society. Also, while my stages correspond to historical periods, my concern is rather with the logical process by which John's anti-structural thinking developed. My state 3 represents the conceptuality of the text as we have it, but I do not deny that the history behind the text is more complicated than the logical process suggests. To address these complications, however, would require us to deal with problems of redaction and tradition that are beyond the scope of this study. My hope is that the results of the study may help others to deal with the complications.

12. See nn. 1 and 10 to the Introduction.

13. Cf. the negations cited in the discussion of the prologue in Chapter 1; others will be observed shortly. In all cases, negation is an anti-posture, and it belongs with synonymy and inversion as characteristics of John's special language.

14. See n. 10, above, and n. 10 to the Introduction.

15. For a broad discussion of the image of Moses in early Judaism and Christianity, see Joachim Jeremias, "Mouses," in Theological Dictionary of the New Testament 4, 848–73. On the image of Moses in John, see T. F. Glasson, Moses in the Fourth Gospel, Studies in Biblical Theology, no. 40 (Naperville: Allenson, 1963); Martyn, History and Theology in the Fourth Gospel, 102–43; and Meeks, The Prophet-King, especially 1–99 and 286–319. I do not think that I have found any Moses material in John that these critics have not observed. Where my discussion differs from theirs is in its orientation to John's anti-structural play with the elements of the image.

16. See Jesus' predictions in 13:19, 14:29, and probably 8:28, for which I am indebted to Meeks, The Prophet-King, 46.

17. See Meeks, The Prophet-King, 290–91, and n. 27, below.

18. See further the section entitled "From Moses to Sophia to Jesus" in Chapter 5, where ascent and descent in Deut. 30:11–20 and Bar. 3:9–4:4 are discussed in relation to John 3:13–21.

19. See Meeks, The Prophet-King, 294.

20. For a detailed discussion, see Peder Borgen, Bread from Heaven: An Exegetical Study of the Concept of Mannah in the Gospel of John and the Writings of Philo, Supplements to Novum Testamentum, vol. 10 (Leiden: Brill, 1965).

21. See Nicholson, Death as Departure, 75–104.

22. On the notion of a Messiah who is understood in terms of the prophet like Moses, see Meeks, The Prophet-King, passim.

23. On the unity of these features as aspects of a notion of mystical ascent, see Meeks, The Prophet-King, 295–301, and "The Man from Heaven in Johannine Sectarianism," 52–53, whom Martyn follows in the revised edition of History and Theology in the Fourth Gospel, 102–43. For further, more recent discussion and literature, see Dunn, "Let John Be John," 306–13.

24. In the section of Chapter 5 entitled "The Only Son of the Father and the Many Sons of Sophia," I will argue that the notion of the "only Son" is anti-structurally derived from the notion of Moses as one of Sophia's sons.

25. in addition to the references in n. 23, above, see those in Chap. 2, n. 29, and Chap. 3, n. 14.

26. See the references cited in n. 23, above.

27. In view of the relationship in John 17 between Jesus' giving God's words, which is derived from Deuteronomy 18, and his revealing of God's name, Meeks sees the notion of the 'name' as derived from God's telling Moses His name in Exod. 3:13–14 and 6:2–3 (The Prophet-King, 290–91, 302–3). However, because of the unity of the Father and

the Son (as, e.g., in John 17:20–21), and because Jesus can say "I am" (4:26; 6:20; 8:24; 28, 58; 13:9; 18:5–6, 8), which is the name God disclosed to Moses, it also appears that the notion of the 'name' is anti-structurally derived from the image of Moses. God revealed His 'name' to Moses, but Jesus appropriated it for himself. For the debate over the "I am" statements, see the references in Chap. 3, n. 3.

28. See Nicholson, *Death as Departure*, 141–51, and the discussion of John 3:1–15, 31–36 in Chapter 2.

29. The notion of Jesus being 'lifted up' or 'exalted' may also be positively informed by the Greek of Isa. 52:13, where the same verb is used in conjunction with the word for 'glorification', which in John is synonymous with 'exaltation'. See, e.g., Barrett, *The Gospel According to St. John*, 214, and more fully, Moloney, *The Johannine Son of Man*, 61–64 (and under references to Isa. 52:13 in the scriptural index). Moloney, however, denies that either term refers to an ascent (see Chap. 2, n. 29).

30. On irony in this story, and on the relationship between the multiple meanings of 'living water', which produces a misunderstanding on the part of the woman, see Duke, *Irony in the Fourth Gospel*, 100–103.

31. See Meeks, *The Prophet-King, passim.*

32. The most comprehensive study of the role of the Law is Severino Pancaro's *The Law in the Fourth Gospel. The Torah and the Gospel: Moses and Jesus, Judaism and Christianity According to John*, Supplements to Novum Testamentum, vol. 42 (Leiden: Brill, 1975).

33. For references, see Meeks, *The Prophet-King*, 65–66 and n. 1.

34. See Meeks, *The Prophet-King*, 294–95, and his notes for references to his discussion of the role of Moses as intercessor in non-Johannine texts.

35. On the relationship between this passage and the next one, John 10, see Meeks, *The Prophet-King*, 66.

36. See ibid., 307–13 (and his notes), and more broadly, Johannes Beutler, S.J., and Robert T. Fortna, eds., *The Shepherd Discourse of John 10 and Its Context*, SNTSMS, 67 (Cambridge: Cambridge University Press, 1991).

Chapter 5. The Prologue Revisited

1. For a broad overview of the Wisdom tradition, the texts, and pertinent secondary literature, see Georg Fohrer and Ulrich Wilckens, "Sophia ktl," in G. Kittel and G. Friedrich, eds., *Theological Dictionary of the New Testament* 7 (1971) 465–526, esp. 489. For a critical discussion of the relationship between Wisdom mythology and the New Testament, which criticizes the idea of a single Wisdom myth, see Elisabeth Schüssler-Fiorenza, "Wisdom Mythology and the Christo-

logical Hymns of the New Testament," in Robert L. Wilken, ed., *Aspects of Wisdom in Judaism and Early Christianity*, University of Notre Dame Center for the Study of Judaism and Christianity in Antiquity, Vol. 1 (Notre Dame: University of Notre Dame, 1975), 17–41. For a comparative view, see C. H. Talbert, "The Myth of a Descending-Ascending Redeemer in Mediterranean Antiquity," *NTS* 22 (1976) 418–40, and for a sociohistorical perspective on the formative stages of later Sophia mythology see Martin Hengel, *Judaism and Hellenism: Studies in Their Encounter in Palestine during the Early Hellenistic Period* 1, trans. John Bowden (Philadelphia: Fortress Press, 1974). On Wisdom/Sophia in John, see e.g., Brown, *The Gospel According to John 1–12*, 122–25, 519–24, and his indices under "Wisdom"; Meeks, "The Man from Heaven in Johannine Sectarianism"; Dunn, "Let John Be John," 314–20; and, on the descent/ascent schema in John, Nicholson, *Death as Departure*. The Wisdom texts themselves are conveniently gathered in Helmer Ringgren, *Word and Wisdom: Studies in the Hypostatization of Divine Qualities and Functions in the Ancient Near East* (Lund: Ohlsson, 1947), with discussion, and George W. E. Nickelsburg and Michael E. Stone, *Faith and Piety in Early Judaism: Texts and Documents* (Philadelphia: Fortress Press, 1983).

2. In Wis. 9:1–2 'word' and 'wisdom' are synonymously paralleled to one another, but in 9:17 God's 'wisdom' is also synonymously paralleled to His 'holy spirit'. For discussion and other parallels, see the works by Brown, Dunn, and Ringgen cited in n. 1, and the commentaries on the notion of 'the Word' in the prologue to John.

3. See the Greek of Sir. 24:8.

4. See above, pp. 97–99.

5. The synoptic parallel in Matt. 11:19 reads "deeds" instead of "children." On the role of Sophia in the Gospels, see James M. Robinson, "Jesus as Sophos and Sophia: Wisdom Tradition and the Gospels," in Wilken, ed., *Aspects of Wisdom in Judaism and Early Christianity*, 1–16.

6. The reference is to the Greek version of Proverbs.

7. In Prov. 7:4 Sophia is referred to as the "sister" of those who follow her, but this is obviously contradicted by the other references to her as a "mother."

8. As persuasively argued by Meeks, *The Prophet-King, passim*.

9. E.g., Meeks, "The Man from Heaven in Johannine Sectarianism," 60; Talbert, "The Myth of a Descending-Ascending Redeemer in Mediterranean Antiquity," 421; and Dunn, "Let John Be John," 314.

10. While wrong about Sophia's alleged descent and ascent, Talbert, "The Myth of a Descending-Ascending Redeemer in Mediterranean Antiquity," 422–40, is correct in seeing the prevalence of these

terms in angel stories. However, he misses the origins of John's use of these terms in the Moses tradition, both in its biblical form and in the Sophia material in Baruch.

11. This story is obviously much different from the extensive Redeemer myth constructed by Bultmann in "Die Bedeutung der neuerschlossenen mandäischen und manichäischen Quellen für das Verständnis des Johannesevangeliums," *ZNW* 24 (1925) 100–146 (reprinted in Bultmann, *Exegetica* [Tübingen: Mohr, 1967], 55–104). For critiques of Bultmann's project, see Meeks, "The Man from Heaven in Johannine Sectarianism," with literature, and of the idea of a single original Wisdom myth, Schüssler-Fiorenza, "Wisdom Mythology and the Christologial Hymns of the New Testament."

12. The contrast between perishing and having eternal life also appears in John 6:27 and 10:28, and in both cases in the context of play with the image of Moses. The contrast and its terms derive from Deuteronomy 30, but John's notion of *eternal* life stands opposed to life in this world, as we saw in connection with John 3:14, 4:13–14, and 6:47–51.

13. Here John anti-structurally inverts what is said of Sophia, while also using anti-language negation.

14. Sophia as "the first-born of creation" is different from Adam being "the first-formed father of the world," whom Sophia "delivered . . . from his transgression and gave . . . strength to rule all things" (Wis. 10:1–2).

15. Rom. 8:29, Phil. 3:20–21, 1 Cor. 15:20–55, on which see further, Petersen, *Rediscovering Paul*, Chap. 3.

16. The translation is by M. A. Knibb, in H. E. D. Sparks, ed., *The Apocryphal Old Testament* (Oxford: Clarendon Press, 1987), 225. For a nonmythological formulation of wisdom's failing to find a "place" in humans, see 1 Enoch 94:5.

17. E.g., Robinson, "Jesus as Sophos and Sophia," 12–13.

18. Proverbs 1–8.

19. Exodus, Deuteronomy.

20. Bar. 3:36.

21. Sir. 24:8.

22. Wis. 10:16. Note that in Wis. 9:10 there is reference to Sophia being 'sent'.

23. John 1:1–18.

24. John 3:16–17.

25. This insight needs to be factored into the sociohistorical picture of developments in the Wisdom tradition sketched by Hengel (see the bibliographical reference in n. 1, above). It is noteworthy that in the earliest Wisdom texts, Proverbs 1–8 and Job 28, there is no reference to

either Moses or the Law, and that such references appear to be added to Sophia material in Sir. 24:23 and Bar. 4:1, presumably by their authors. Likewise, the Law is not mentioned in the Wisdom material in Wisdom 1 and 6–11, not even in connection with Moses in 10:15–19:22. Admittedly, the references to events in Exodus ends before the giving of the Law, but it is still striking that the Law is not mentioned (the reference to the "laws" of Sophia in 6:18 appears to be related to wise instruction). In this light, Sirach and Baruch on the one hand, and Wisdom of Solomon on the other, reflect different developments of earlier Sophia material that lacked reference to Moses and the Law. And in both cases Moses' role is subordinated to Sophia's. John 1:1–18, because it refers to Moses and the Law in connection with Sophia material, reflects knowledge of the developments represented in Sirach and Baruch, but also, as seen above, of developments represented in the Wisdom of Solomon.

26. Some of these modifications are informed by pre-Johannine Jesus traditions and the social history of John's people. On these matters, see the references in n. 4 to the Introduction.

27. The point is well argued by Nicholson, *Death as Departure*.

28. See n. 25, above.

29. See Wilckens, *"Sophia ktl,"* and the essays in Wilken, *Aspects of Wisdom in Judaism and Early Christianity*.

Scriptural Index

Made in the USA
Middletown, DE
12 February 2021